C000136195

Pass your

Numeracy and Literacy Skills Test

Revision and Practice for your QTS
Skills Tests

Sam Kirkwood

Lewis Wilding

Oliver Naylor

TABLE OF CONTENTS

QTS LITERACY TUTOR
WWW.LITERACYSKILLSTEST.CO.UK

FREE ONLINE LITERACY SKILLS TEST
EXPERT 1 TO 1 TUITION WITH OUR QTS SPECIALISTS

— WHAT QTS LITERACY TUTOR HAS TO OFFER —

Spelling Practice

Punctuation Questions

Grammar Section

Comprehension Resources

Practice Tests

Expert Tutors

Correct Format

New Question Formats

Visit www.literacyskillstest.co.uk to take a Free Full Practice Test today.

10
LITERACY SKILLS TESTS

97%
LEARNER PASS RATE

490
TEST QUESTIONS

About the authors

This QTS skills test book has been produced through a collaboration of industry experts. A team of numeracy and literacy skills tutors, mathematicians and expert teachers have devised a comprehensive QTS skills book that covers all aspects of both tests, including the most up to date question types.

As part of the book, there are also links to other resources such as **videos** and **practice tests** that are regularly updated, making sure that the book remains more relevant than any others out there. The tutors and experts who have collaborated on the book have first-hand experience of what people struggle with when preparing for their QTS tests. This book has been designed from the student's perspective making the hints, tips and learning resources even more effective.

Our team provides the leading QTS skills practice test and tuition service in the country and this experience is reflected in the contents of this book.

Visit **https://www.QTSMathsTutor.co.uk/QTSSkillsTest/** to access more numeracy and literacy skills resources and practice tests.

QTS Numeracy Skills Test

The numeracy skills test comprises of two sections, a mental arithmetic section followed by a written data section. The 12 mental arithmetic questions require you to calculate your answers within 18 seconds of the second repeat of the question. You must answer all 12 questions in a row and there is no option to go back. You are not permitted to use a calculator in this part of the test.

The written section is made up of 16 onscreen graph and data questions. You have a total of 36 minutes to answer questions 13 to 28 which are based on graphs, tables and data interpretation. You are permitted to use an onscreen calculator in this part of the test.

Both sections of the test require you to submit your answer onscreen, very similar to the QTS Maths Tutor interactive tests and the government practice tests which you can find online using the website links below. Many people ask, what is the pass mark for the numeracy skills test? The answer is it changes depending on the difficulty of the test. The average pass mark appears to be around 18, or 63%. Whilst doing the practice numeracy skills tests, we advise that you aim to achieve 20 or more to be confident in passing the real exam.

There is more information about the skills tests, common mistakes, testing centres and much more at: **www.QTSMathsTutor.co.uk** and **http://sta.education.gov.uk/**.

QTS Maths Tutor Help Sheet

The following conversions, formulae and tips are a really good starting point to help you with the most common types of maths questions that appear in the numeracy skills test.

Fractions	Percentages	Decimals
$\frac{1}{2}$	50%	0.5
$\frac{1}{3}$	33.$\dot{3}$%	0.$\dot{3}$
$\frac{2}{3}$	66.$\dot{6}$%	0.$\dot{6}$
$\frac{1}{4}$	25%	0.25
$\frac{3}{4}$	75%	0.75
$\frac{1}{5}$	20%	0.2
$\frac{1}{8}$	12.5%	0.125
$\frac{1}{10}$	10%	0.1
$\frac{1}{20}$	5%	0.05

Percentage and Fractions

Calculate percentage of an amount:	$= \left(\dfrac{Amount}{Original}\right) \times 100$
Percentage Increase:	$= \left(\dfrac{Increase}{Original}\right) \times 100$
Percentage Decrease	$= \left(\dfrac{Decrease}{Original}\right) \times 100$
Fraction of an amount:	$= Fraction \times Amount$

Multiplication and Division tricks

× 4	*× 2 then × 2 again*
÷ 4	*÷ 2 then ÷ 2 again*
× 10	*Move the decimal point 1 place to the right*
÷ 10	*Move the decimal point 1 place to the left*
÷ 0.1	*× 10*
× 0.1	*÷ 10*
÷ 0.2	*÷ 2 then × 10*
× 0.2	*× 2 then ÷ 10*
÷ 0.25	*× 4*
× 0.25	*÷ 4*
÷ 0.5	*× 2*
× 0.5	*÷ 2*

Mean, Mode , Median and Range

Finding the mean:	$= \dfrac{Add\ up\ all\ the\ numbers}{How\ many\ numbers\ there\ are}$
Finding the range of a set:	$= Highest\ in\ a\ set - Lowest\ in\ the\ set$
Finding the median:	*Put the set in ascending order then find the* $\dfrac{n+1}{2}^{th}$ *term.*
Finding the mode:	$= Most\ common\ term\ in\ set.$

Mental Arithmetic Section (Non-Calculator)

Mental arithmetic questions are often the questions that people are most fearful of. This is due to the pressure created by the **18 second time limit** which is applied to every question.

The clock starts ticking after the second repeat of the question and if you aren't confident with your mental maths, then this can be quite daunting. This section of the book comprehensively covers all of the mental arithmetic question types and topics that come up in the test.

You can use the guidance notes along with the practice and exam style questions to help you develop the methods and techniques required to successfully navigate this part of the exam.

From fractions to percentages, everything is covered and many of the skills needed are also applicable to the written data section so it is important to learn the methods and get plenty of practise using them. To practise questions in the audio format like the actual test we recommend you visit the QTS Maths Tutor website.

1. Multiplication

1.1 I can multiply numbers from 1 to 12 - SKILLS Questions

a)	9 × 12	g)	11 × 2	m)	12 × 3 × 4
b)	3 × 8	h)	4 × 4 × 11	n)	6 × 11 × 6
c)	5 × 3	i)	10 × 2 × 12	o)	4 × 4 × 10
d)	11 × 6	j)	5 × 7 × 8	p)	3 × 11 × 10
e)	6 × 10	k)	7 × 9 × 2	q)	4 × 12 × 12
f)	3 × 11	l)	4 × 11 × 9	r)	10× 10 × 2

1.2 I can multiply numbers from 1 to 12 - TEST Questions

a) Four students each run 5 kilometres on a Tuesday and 7 kilometres on every other day of the week. How many kilometres do the students run altogether in a week?

b) At Brownhill Academy four teachers set 3 pieces of homework to each pupil in their class. If the average class size is 12, how many pieces of homework were set in total?

c) Three teaching assistants each read 4 articles on a Thursday and 6 on a Monday. How many articles are read by the teaching assistants in one week?

d) Three teachers each read 4 books on 7 different occasions. How many books do the teachers read altogether?

e) Three teachers purchase 2 pencils for each of the students in their class. If on average each class contains 11 pupils, how many pencils were bought in total?

f) A teacher reads over 4 sample exams for each of the pupils in his revision class separately. If there are 8 students in the class, how many sample exams does the teacher read?

g) Seven pupils each eat 2 bags of crisps, one sandwich and two chocolate bars. Altogether, how many items of food do the pupils eat?

h) At Langwith College a student reads 3 research papers on a Monday, Tuesday, Friday, Saturday and Sunday and 6 on each of the remaining days of the week. In one week, how many research papers does the student read?

i) Three pupils each eat 5 sweets on each day of the weekend. How many sweets do the pupils eat altogether?

j) Four teachers each drink two bottles of water containing 3 litres per bottle. How much water do they drink altogether? Give your answer in litres.

1.3 I can use the grid multiplication method
Introduction

There was a time when written multiplication was done in columns. This has now been replaced by the grid method of multiplication which has been part of primary school teaching since the 90s. This method requires less attention on the size of the number, i.e. how many zeros you add at the end, and this reduces the scope for error. Whether you use this method or the column method for the test you will need to know the grid method when working through your teacher training course.

Multiplication by 10, 100, 1000

To perform grid multiplication quickly it is necessary to know how to multiply 10s, 100s and 1000s together.

1. What is **100 × 200**? Well, do 1 × 2 = 2 and as there are 4 zeros in the question, stick on 4 zeros in the answer (0000). Therefore, **100 × 200 =** 20000.

2. What is **30 × 500**? Well, 3 × 5 = 15 and there are 3 zeros in the question, stick on 3 zeros in the answer (000). Therefore, **30 × 500 =** 15000.

Explanation Example

Example 1

What is **12 × 3**?

1. Break up the numbers and write them out in a grid.

2. Complete the grid by multiplying the numbers together.

3. Add up the numbers and this is the answer.

$$12 \times 3$$
$$(10 + 2) \times 3$$

×	3
10	30
2	6

$$30 + 6 = 36$$
$$12 \times 3 = 36$$

Example 2

What is **79 × 45**?

1. Break up the numbers and write them out in a grid.

2. Complete the grid by multiplying the numbers together.

3. Add up the numbers, writing them in columns for ease, and get your final answer.

$$79 \times 45$$
$$(70 + 9) \times (40 + 5)$$

×	40	5	Sum
70	2800	350	3150
9	360	45	405 +
			3555

$$79 \times 45 = 3555$$

Example 3: Test Question

A teacher needs **71** pieces of paper per pupil. There are **40** pupils. How many pieces are needed in total?

$$71 \times 40$$

×	70	1	Sum
40	2800	40	2840

$$71 \times 40 = 2840$$

Example 4: Test Question

A teacher needs **79** millilitres of milk for every student. The class has **34** students. How many millilitres of milk are needed altogether?

$$79 \times 34$$

×	70	9	Sum
30	2100	270	2370
4	280	36	316
			2686

$79 \times 34 = 2686$ mm

1.4   I can use the grid multiplication method - SKILLS Questions

a)	42×4	g)	764×75	m)	5401×243
b)	80×48	h)	217×122	n)	5550×2902
c)	80×71	i)	799×572	o)	7638×5562
d)	26×44	j)	896×777	p)	97606×5
e)	45×15	k)	6481×7	q)	84714×71
f)	785×6	l)	8106×51	r)	74718×972

Need to practise!

1.5   I can use the grid multiplication method - TEST Questions ✓

a)   Two teachers each order 38 leaflets, each leaflet costs 38 pence. How much did they spend in total? Give your answer in pounds.

b)   Two teachers in a school each buy 23 rulers, each ruler costs 24 pence. How much did they spend in total? Give your answer in pounds.

c)   A school requires 61 exercise books per pupil during their school life. If a class has 60 pupils, how many exercise books are required altogether?

d)   Two Principals in the West Midlands each order 14 posters. Another four Principals order 26 posters. How many posters did the Principals order in total?

e)   A pupil in a drama group travels 28 miles to another school, each mile costs 15 pence in fuel. How much did the pupil spend on fuel? Give your answer in pounds.

f)   28 teachers in a school each buy 17 books. 3 teachers buy 18 books. How many books did the teachers buy in total?

g)   Three parents each order 37 Christmas cards. A further 2 parents order 16 Christmas cards. How many Christmas cards did the parents order in total?

h)   Two departments each buy 25 books. A further 3 departments buy 25 books. How many books did the different departments buy?

i)   Two students each spend £15.75 on their history revision guides. How much do the students spend in total purchasing their history revision guides? Give your answer in pounds.

j)   On average students use 29 pieces of stationery during a school year. If a class has 35 students, how many pieces of stationery are used in total during one school year?

1.6   I can multiply by fractions

Introduction

The multiplication of fractions is one of the easier techniques to master as it involves multiplying the tops of the fractions (numerators) together and the bottoms (denominators) together. After this, sometimes it is possible to reduce the fraction to its simplest (or lowest) form.

You will need to know how to multiply numbers together, how to reduce fractions to their simplest form and be aware that whole numbers can be written as fractions with 1 on the bottom. For example 2 is the same as $\frac{2}{1}$.

You should note that the word 'of' in mathematics means multiply. For example, 10 lots **of** 2 bananas = **10 × 2 = 20** bananas.

Explanation Example

Example 1

What is $\frac{1}{2} \times \frac{1}{2}$?

1. Multiply the tops.
2. Multiply the bottoms.
3. Simplify if needed

$$\frac{1}{2} \times \frac{1}{2} = \frac{1}{4}$$

Example 2

What is $\frac{2}{3} \times \frac{1}{5}$?

1. Multiply the tops.
2. Multiply the bottoms.
3. Simplify if needed.

$$\frac{2}{3} \times \frac{1}{5} = \frac{2}{15}$$

In this instance we cannot simplify it.

Example 3

What is $\frac{2}{4} \times \frac{2}{8}$?

1. Multiply the tops.
2. Multiply the bottoms.
3. Simplify.

$$\frac{2}{4} \times \frac{2}{8} = \frac{1}{8}$$

$$\frac{2}{4} \times \frac{2}{8} = \frac{4}{32}$$

÷4

$$\frac{4}{32} = \frac{1}{8}$$

÷4

Example 4: Test Question

In a year group of **96** children, $\frac{3}{4}$ of them took part in a sports day. How many of the year group did **not** take part in the sports day?

(Remember if ¾ take part, ¼ don't take part)

$$\frac{1}{4} \ of \ 96 = 24$$

$$\frac{1}{4} \times \frac{96}{1} = \frac{96}{4}$$

÷4

$$\frac{96}{4} = \frac{24}{1} = 24$$

÷4

1.7   I can multiply by fractions – SKILLS Questions

a) $\dfrac{1}{2} \times \dfrac{1}{3}$ e) $\dfrac{1}{3} \times \dfrac{2}{8}$ i) $\dfrac{6}{7} \times \dfrac{6}{7}$ m) $\dfrac{1}{3} \times 99$ q) $\dfrac{2}{6} \times 66$

b) $\dfrac{1}{6} \times \dfrac{1}{4}$ f) $\dfrac{3}{7} \times \dfrac{4}{6}$ j) $\dfrac{1}{9} \times \dfrac{1}{1}$ n) $\dfrac{1}{5} \times 125$ r) $\dfrac{3}{8} \times 40$

c) $\dfrac{1}{3} \times \dfrac{1}{6}$ g) $\dfrac{7}{9} \times \dfrac{1}{3}$ k) $\dfrac{1}{2} \times 30$ o) $\dfrac{1}{8} \times 200$

d) $\dfrac{2}{3} \times \dfrac{2}{5}$ h) $\dfrac{8}{9} \times \dfrac{2}{5}$ l) $\dfrac{1}{4} \times 100$ p) $\dfrac{2}{3} \times 66$

1.8   I can multiply by fractions – TEST Questions

a) The total cost of a school trip is £350 per pupil. $\dfrac{1}{10}$ of this cost is travel, which is covered by the school. How much will each pupil have to pay if they have to pay the remaining amount?

b) In an English exam $\dfrac{2}{8}$ of the marks were from a poetry test and $\dfrac{6}{8}$ from prose coursework. In the poetry test, $\dfrac{6}{7}$ of the marks were for spelling and punctuation. What fraction of the marks for the overall English exam was from spelling and punctuation?

c) In a school with 1200 students, $\dfrac{1}{12}$ passed the English exam. How many students passed the English exam?

d) In a rowing team $\dfrac{3}{6}$ of the team were boys and $\dfrac{3}{6}$ were girls. Of the boys, $\dfrac{2}{8}$ were A-Level students. What fraction of the rowing team were A-Level students?

e) In a French exam $\frac{6}{10}$ of the marks were from an oral exam and $\frac{4}{10}$ from a reading paper. In the oral exam, $\frac{2}{10}$ of the marks were from knowledge of nouns. What fraction of the total mark was from knowledge of nouns?

f) An assessment of 500 school chairs found that $\frac{10}{100}$ were damaged and would need replacing. How many chairs need replacing?

g) In a school with 250 pupils, $\frac{20}{100}$ achieved a Grade 5. What number of the school did not achieve a Grade 5?

h) In a class of 15 students, $\frac{4}{5}$ failed an exam. How many students failed?

i) In a group of 200 students, $\frac{1}{8}$ achieved a GCSE Grade 7. How many of the group achieved a GCSE Grade 7?

j) In a Literature exam $\frac{3}{6}$ of the marks were from a poetry test and $\frac{3}{6}$ from prose coursework. In the poetry test, $\frac{7}{8}$ of the marks were from grammar. What fraction of the Literature exam marks was from grammar?

1.9   I can multiply by decimals

Introduction

The method we will use to multiply decimals is explained using examples. It will require knowledge of the grid method of multiplication, which is described in section 1.3 on page 13. These can be very tricky under the time pressure of the real exam so make sure you get lots of practice.

Explanation Example

Example 1

What is **0.5 × 1.1**?

1. Ignore the decimals and convert the numbers into whole numbers.

2. Perform grid multiplication.

3. Go back to the original question and count up the amount of numbers after every decimal point.

4. You need the same number of figures after the decimal in your answer from part **2** (count from the right).

5 ×11

×	10	1	
5	50	5	55

What is 0.5 × 1.1?

55

Move 2 decimal places

0.5 × 1.1 = 0.55

Example 2: Test Question

A head teacher needs **4.3** litres of milk for each pupil. There are **3** pupils. How many litres are needed in total?

$$4.3 \times 3$$

$$43 \times 3$$

×	40	3	
3	120	9	129

What is 4.3 × 3?

12.9 litres of milk

Example 3: Test Question

What is **0.03 × 4.5**?

1. Ignore the decimals

$$00.3 \times 45$$
$$3 \times 45$$

2. Perform grid multiplication.

×	40	5	
3	120	15	135

3. Go back to the original question and count up the amount of numbers after every decimal point.

What is 0.03 × 4.5?

135

4. You need the same number of figures after the decimal in your answer from part **2.**
(Count from the right).

Move 3 decimal places

$$0.03 \times 4.5 = 0.135$$

Example 4: Test Question

A teaching assistant needs **3.25** centimetres of paper for each pupil. There are **6** pupils. How many centimetres are needed altogether?

3.25 × 6
325 × 6

×	300	20	5	
6	1800	120	30	1950

What is 3.25 × 6 ?
1950
19.5 cm of paper

1.10   I can multiply by decimals – SKILLS Questions

a)	1 × 0.1	g)	0.002 × 6.2	m)	5.4 × 5.8
b)	87 × 3.1	h)	0.125 × 3	n)	1.72 × 0.53
c)	64 × 1.2	i)	6.4 × 4.1	o)	4.61 × 7.88
d)	13.1 × 0.2	j)	5.5 × 1.5	p)	0.22 × 0.86
e)	0.5 × 0.5	k)	6.5 × 6	q)	0.93 × 5.86
f)	10 × 0.1	l)	8.9 × 6.3	r)	0.94 × 4.72

1.11   I can multiply by decimals – TEST Questions

a) A teacher buys 5 boxes for storage. Each box holds 6.6 kilograms. How many kilograms do the boxes hold altogether?

b) A technology teacher requires an average of 2.5 items per student for a project they are undertaking. If there are 20 pupils in the class, how many items are needed for the project?

c)   On average a teacher requires 3.5 pieces of paper for each pupil in her class. There are 20 pupils in her class. How many pieces of paper does she need?

d)   A classroom requires 7 pieces of carpet to replace the damage. Using the fact that one piece measures 10.45 metres, what is the amount required in total?

e)   A teacher runs 3 circuits a week. Knowing that one complete circuit is 11.9 kilometres, what is the number of kilometres ran altogether?

f)   A science teacher needs 3.4 millilitres of vinegar for each student. The class has 4 students. How many millilitres are needed in total?

g)   A bench requires 2 pieces of identical wood. Knowing that one-piece measures 2.15 metres, what is the total amount of wood required?

h)   A child buys 8 boxes of toys. Using the fact that one box holds 2.85 kilograms, what is the weight of the boxes in total?

i)   A school badminton team buys 1.9 litres of juice per student. There are 5 students in the badminton team. How many litres of juice are purchased?

j)   A school requires 4.25 centimetres of rope for each pupil. There are 12 pupils. How many centimetres are required in total?

2. Division

Introduction

To succeed at division based questions you need to be confident with your multiplication ability, especially your times tables from 1 to 12. **See Page 12 for more help with this.**

Division is the opposite operation to multiplication.

Asking

> What do we get if we divide 42 by 6?

Has the same solution as asking

> What do we have to multiply by 6 to get 42?

In both instances the answer is 7.

A standard method of performing written division is the 'bus stop' method which is shown in the following examples.

Explanation Example

Example 1

What is **125 ÷ 5**?

(How many 5s go into 125?)

1. Set it out in using the bus stop method

$$\text{e.g. } 5 \overline{\smash{)}125}$$

2. Then go through asking the following questions:

3. **How many times does 5 go into 12?** Twice. Put a 2 on top. It has remainder 2, carry it over and bring the remainder you haven't yet used down to create a new number, 25.

$$\text{e.g. } 5 \overline{\smash{)}1\,2^2 5}$$

4. How many times does 5 go into 25?

Five. Put a 5 on top. No remainder. As we have nothing else to divide we can stop.

So the answer is **25**.

$$\text{e.g. } 5\overline{)1\,2\,^25} \quad 2\,5$$

Example 2: Test Question

The total distance of a cross country run was **27** miles. The run consisted of **4** laps around a route. How long was one lap?

$$27 \div 4$$

$$4\overline{)2\,^27.\,^30\,^20} \quad 0\,6\,.\,7\,5$$

27 miles ÷ 4 = 6.75 miles

Example 3: Test Question

Teachers at Forest Academy spend **135** pounds on travel. The total amount is equally split between **6** trips. What is the cost of each trip?

$$135 \div 6$$

$$6\overline{)1\,^13\,^15.\,^30\,0} \quad 0\,2\,2\,.\,5$$

£135 ÷ 6 = £22.50

2.1 I can perform division using the standard method – SKILLS Questions

Find solutions to the following, giving your answer to 2 decimal places where required.

a)	$5 \div 4$	g)	$45 \div 4$	m)	$156 \div 12$
b)	$9 \div 8$	h)	$95 \div 6$	n)	$487 \div 20$
c)	$6 \div 4$	i)	$74 \div 8$	o)	$519 \div 3$
d)	$4 \div 1$	j)	$15 \div 9$	p)	$561 \div 5$
e)	$10 \div 10$	k)	$46 \div 4$	q)	$498 \div 4$
f)	$52 \div 15$	l)	$154 \div 5$	r)	$1054 \div 6$

2.2 I can perform division using the standard method – TEST Questions

a) The staff members at River Community School have 339.5 litres of paint. This is the total amount needed for 7 days of events at a nursery. How much paint is needed for one day?

b) A group of pupils cycle 213.5 miles in preparation for regional trials. The total distance is made up of 7 laps around the country route. What is the distance of one lap?

c) A food technology department had 192.5 litres of milk. The total volume was used during 7 days of baking. What was the volume used in one day assuming that an equal amount was used each day?

d) A school bought 138 pieces of computer equipment. The equipment is equally shared between four computer suites. How many pieces of equipment did each room get?

e) The librarian at St Cuthbert's buys three sets of books for a total of £72. Each set cost the same amount. How much does one set cost?

f) Fifteen school teachers drink a total of 30 litres of coffee during one month. How much does one teacher drink, assuming they all drink the same amount?

g) Ten pupils carry 75 kilograms of equipment. How much does each pupil carry on average?

h) The entry to a museum cost £140 for seventy pupils. How much did one ticket cost?

i) Twenty pupils carry a total of 180 kilograms worth of equipment for their school's sports day. If each pupil carries the same amount, how much does each pupil carry?

j) Ninety parents pay a total of £765 pounds for their child's school trip. How much does each parent pay?

2.3   I can solve decimal division - Introduction

The method we will use to divide decimals is explained using examples. It will require knowledge of the short division method demonstrated below.

If dividing with a decimal we need to multiply by a factor of 10 (10, 100, 1000, 10000 etc....) to get rid of the decimal- as it is easier to work with whole numbers.

Explanation Example

Example 1

What is **6 ÷ 0.5** ?

$$6 \div 0.5$$

1. Multiply both numbers by **10**.

$$6 \times 10 \div 0.5 \times 10$$

2. Perform the division. So divide by 5

3. This gives the answer of 12

$$60 \div 5$$

$$12$$

Example 2

What is **10 ÷ 0.05?**

1. Multiply both numbers by **100** to make the division easier.

2. Perform the division.

$$10 ÷ 0.05$$
$$10 × 100 ÷ 0.05 × 100$$
$$1000 ÷ 5$$
$$200$$

Example 3: Test Question

What is **0.2 ÷ 20?**

1. This example is different as the number you are dividing is a decimal.

2. Perform the division **0.2 divided by 2 which is 0.1** and then move the decimal place 1 to the left as you are dividing by 20 instead of 2. For every extra **0** you move the decimal place by one.

$$0.2 ÷ 2 = 0.1$$
$$0.2 ÷ 20$$
$$0.01$$

Example 4 Test Question

What is **0.01 ÷ 0.008?**

1. Multiply both numbers by **1000** to make the division easier.

2. Perform the division.

$$0.01 ÷ 0.008$$
$$0.01 × 1000 ÷ 0.008 × 1000$$
$$10 ÷ 8$$
$$1.25$$

2.4   I can solve decimal division questions – SKILLS Questions

a)	1.5 ÷ 5	g)	16 ÷ 0.04	m)	5656 ÷ 0.8
b)	2.6 ÷ 3	h)	12.6 ÷ 1.2	n)	4 ÷ 0.0002
c)	11.2 ÷ 4	i)	99 ÷ 0.03	o)	0.16 ÷ 0.16
d)	5.5 ÷ 0.5	j)	100 ÷ 0.8	p)	0.7 ÷ 0.002
e)	7.2 ÷ 0.9	k)	1.65 ÷ 0.3	q)	10 ÷ 0.25
f)	0.25 ÷ 0.05	l)	6 ÷ 0.006	r)	1 ÷ 0.7

2.5   I can solve decimal division questions – TEST Questions

a) What is two hundred and forty-three divided by zero point zero one?

b) What is eight thousand two hundred and forty-seven divided by zero point two?

c) What is one thousand six hundred and forty-six divided by zero point two?

d) What is seven hundred and twenty-nine divided by zero point zero one?

e) What is twenty-seven thousand four hundred and thirty-five divided by zero point zero one?

f) What is fifteen thousand eight hundred and forty divided by zero point three?

g) What is one thousand two hundred and sixty-six divided by zero point one?

h) What is nine thousand forty-three divided by zero point two?

i) What is five hundred and ninety-three divided by zero point two?

j) What is six thousand one hundred and sixty-eight divided by zero point three?

3. Fractions

Introduction to simplifying fractions

Write your answer in its simplest form, are words that often appear on the skills test. This means if you have a fraction you need to write it such that the top and bottom numbers cannot be divided by the same number any further.

In the rectangle below $\frac{6}{18}$ squares have been shaded in. However we can simplify this fraction, by dividing top and bottom by 6:

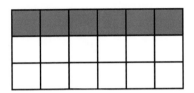

This gives us $\frac{1}{3}$ which we can see is true from looking at the diagram as 1 in every 3 squares is blue.

Explanation Example

Example 1

Simplify $\frac{4}{8}$

1. Find what number you can divide 4 and 8 by.

    4

2. Divide the top by 4.

3. Divide the bottom by 4.

4. Can we divide it any further?

    No

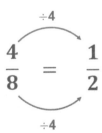

Example 2

Simplify $\frac{66}{110}$

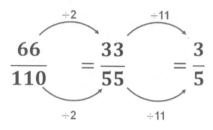

1. As both of these numbers are even we can divide by 2.

2. Both of these numbers aren't even. They are both divisible by 11.

Example 3: Test Question

In a year with **18** students, **3** passed the English exam. What fraction of the year passed the English exam? Give your answer in its lowest terms.

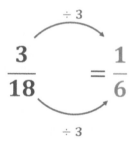

Example 4: Test Question

In a year with **45** pupils, **72** passed the English exam.

What fraction of the year did **not** pass the English exam? Give your answer in its lowest terms.

72 − 45 = 27 *didn't pass*

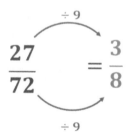

3.1   I can simplify fractions – SKILLS Questions

Simplify the following fractions.

a)	$\dfrac{4}{8}$	f)	$\dfrac{2}{14}$	k)	$\dfrac{2}{24}$	o)	$\dfrac{18}{81}$
b)	$\dfrac{2}{18}$	g)	$\dfrac{4}{12}$	l)	$\dfrac{20}{30}$	p)	$\dfrac{16}{88}$
c)	$\dfrac{3}{12}$	h)	$\dfrac{2}{10}$	m)	$\dfrac{22}{77}$	q)	$\dfrac{27}{45}$
d)	$\dfrac{11}{110}$	i)	$\dfrac{5}{55}$	n)	$\dfrac{20}{50}$	r)	$\dfrac{25}{35}$
e)	$\dfrac{7}{42}$	j)	$\dfrac{4}{32}$				

3.2   I can simplify fractions – TEST Questions

a)   In a class of 36 children, 9 were boys. What fraction of the class were boys? Give your answer in its lowest terms.

b)   In a gym with 350 members, only 35 were above the age of 60. What fraction of the members were below the age of 60? Give your answer in its lowest terms.

c)   In a year of 63 children, 18 passed the English exam. What fraction of the year did not pass the English exam? Give your answer in its lowest terms.

d)   Eleven out of 33 pupils in a class needed additional support. What fraction of the class did not need additional support? Give your answer in its lowest terms.

e) Out of 150 pupils, 15 needed to wear glasses. What fraction of the school did not need to wear glasses? Give your answer in its lowest terms.

f) In a class of 36 pupils, 9 take part in the sports day. What fraction of the class did not take part in the sports day? Give your answer in its lowest terms.

g) In a group of 35 pupils, 15 preferred maths to English. What fraction of the group preferred English to maths? Give your answer in its lowest terms.

h) Fifty out of 750 children obtained a Grade 9 at GCSE. What proportion of the children achieved a Grade 9? Give your answer as fraction in its lowest terms.

i) In a school of 300 children, 20 students were deemed as excelling beyond their years; what fraction of the school was this? Give your answer in its lowest terms.

j) In a year with 42 pupils, 35 took part in the sports day. Writing your answer as a fraction in its simplest form, what proportion took part in the sports day?

3.3 Convert between fractions, decimals and percentages
Introduction

Of the twelve mental arithmetic questions, it is likely that a conversion between fractions, decimals and percentages (FDP) will come up. It will therefore be useful to memorise some conversions and practice converting from one to the other. View some key fractions, decimals and percentages on **page 7**. Once you have learnt these, other FDP conversions can be calculated using them.

There are two different methods for completing FDP conversions:

1. You can cancel fractions down, making it easier to convert them once you have learnt the basic conversions.

2. An alternative method is to make the denominator (bottom number) equal 100, the top number will then be equal to that number as a percentage. (e.g. $\frac{57}{100} = 57\%$)

Explanation Example

Example 1: Convert $\frac{16}{20}$ into a percentage.

Example 1: Method 1

1. Cancel the fraction down by dividing the top and bottom by 4.

2. Using your knowledge of fractions. $\frac{1}{5} = 20\%$ we can then convert the result into a percentage as shown.

$$\div 4$$
$$\frac{16}{20} = \frac{4}{5}$$
$$\div 4$$

Using this method

$$\frac{4}{5} = 80\%$$

Example 1: Method 2

1. The aim of this method is to get the bottom number to 100. To do this we multiply both numbers by 5.

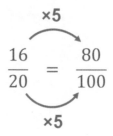

2. When any fraction is written with the bottom number as 100 the top number will equal the percentage. Using this we can calculate the percentage.

Using this method

$$\frac{80}{100} = 80\%$$

Example 2:

Convert 0.96 to a percentage.

1. You simply multiply by 100 to convert from a decimal into a percentage.

$$0.96 \times 100 = 96\%$$

Example 3: Test Question

In a class of 18 pupils, **12** passed the English exam. What proportion of the class failed the English exam? Give your answer as decimal.

$\div 3$

$$\frac{6}{18} = \frac{1}{3}$$

$\div 3$

$$\frac{1}{3} = 0.33$$

Example 4: Test Question

In a reception class of 25 students, **5** were performing well above average. What percentage of the class performed well above average?

$$\overset{\times 4}{\underset{\times 4}{\frac{5}{25} = \frac{20}{100}}}$$

Using your conversion knowledge

$$\frac{20}{100} = 20\%$$

3.4 I can convert between fractions, decimals and percentages – SKILLS Questions

Write each of the following fractions as a decimal and a percentage.

a)	$\frac{1}{2}$	f)	$\frac{1}{7}$	k)	$\frac{3}{5}$	o)	$\frac{3}{4}$
b)	$\frac{1}{3}$	g)	$\frac{1}{8}$	l)	$\frac{4}{10}$	p)	$\frac{2}{3}$
c)	$\frac{1}{4}$	h)	$\frac{1}{10}$	m)	$\frac{3}{25}$	q)	$\frac{68}{200}$
d)	$\frac{1}{5}$	i)	$\frac{1}{25}$	n)	$\frac{16}{50}$	r)	$\frac{24}{120}$
e)	$\frac{1}{6}$	j)	$\frac{1}{50}$				

3.5   I can convert between fractions, decimals and percentages – TEST Questions

a) A school's senior management team was made up of 27 people above the age of 40 and only 3 people below this age. What proportion of the senior management team was below the age of 40? Give your answer as a decimal.

b) In a school of 150 people, 15 were teachers. What proportion of the school were not teachers? Give your answer as a percentage.

c) In a class of 36 students, 6 of the students had brown hair. What proportion of the class did not have brown hair? Give your answer as a decimal.

d) Two thirds of a Physical Education class selected football as their first choice of activity. What proportion did not choose football? Give your answer as a decimal.

e) 60 students were assessed for their maths ability in comparison to the national average for their age group, 15 were found to be under achieving. What proportion of the students was under achieving? Give your answer as a decimal.

f) Out of 480 pupils, 60 needed additional support. What proportion of the group did not need additional support? Give your answer as a percentage.

g) In a year of 150 students, 25 achieved an A* grade in their recent history exam. What proportion of the year achieved the highest grade? Give your answer as a decimal.

h) Out of 275 students, 55 said they enjoyed Art. What proportion of the students enjoyed Art? Give your answer as a decimal.

i) A school teacher bought pens, pencils and rulers for her class. Out of the 64 pieces of stationery she bought, 8 of them were pencils. What percentage of the stationery were pencils?

j) From a primary school of 600 pupils, 60 take part in the sports day. What proportion of the school take part in the sports day? Give your answer as a percentage.

3.6   I can calculate a fraction of an amount

Introduction

There are many proportion questions on the mental arithmetic section of the test and these can be applied to various contexts. The questions vary the proportion from fractions to decimals to percentages. We recommend taking another look at multiplying by fractions on **page 17**, multiplying decimals on **page 21** and converting between fraction, decimals and percentages on **page 35**.

Note: the word **of** in mathematics means × **(times)**.

Explanation Example

Example 1

Find $\frac{2}{5}$ of 20. $\frac{1}{5}$ of 20

1. Splitting 20 into fifths gives us 4.

   $20 \div 5 \times 1 = 4$

2. Therefore one fifth is 4.

3. Find $\frac{2}{5}$ of 20.

   $\frac{2}{5}$ of 20

The method is: divide by the bottom of the fraction (denominator) and times by the top (numerator). $20 \div 5 \times 2 = 8$

39

Example 2

Find 40% of 60.

$$10\% = 60 \div 10 = 6$$

$$40\% = 4 \times 10\% = 4 \times 6 = 24$$

1. Find 10% by dividing the amount by 10.
2. Find 40% by multiplying 6 by 4.

40% of 60 is 24

Example 3

Find 0.25 of 20.

Convert this to the fraction $\frac{1}{4}$ or a percentage 25% and use the method you feel most comfortable with.

$$20 \div 4 \times 1 = 5$$

0.25 of 20 = 5

Example 4: Test Question

In a class with **40** pupils, $\frac{2}{10}$ passed their English exam. How many people in the class passed their English exam?

$$40 \div 10 = 4$$

$$4 \times 2 = 8$$

8 pupils passed the English exam

Example 5: Test Question

The total cost of a coach for a school trip came to **140** pounds, **25%** was charged to the parents. How much did the parents pay?

$$25\% = \frac{1}{4}$$

$\frac{1}{4}$ of 140

$$140 \div 4 = 35$$

25% of 140 is £35

Note: Fraction of an amount questions are given in section 1.7 on **page 19.**

3.7   I can calculate a proportion of an amount - SKILLS Questions

a)	45% of 175	g)	45% of 740	m)	0.9 of 405
b)	80% of 65	h)	0.25 of 780	n)	50% of 15
c)	0.05 of 325	i)	0.15 of 330	o)	40% of 595
d)	15% of 565	j)	0.35 of 575	p)	75% of 360
e)	0.65 of 400	k)	0.85 of 255	q)	60% of 285
f)	40% of 650	l)	0.6 of 455	r)	40% of 955

3.8   I can calculate a proportion of an amount – TEST Questions

a) In a class with 24 pupils, $\frac{1}{3}$ took part in the sports day. How many pupils in the class did not take part in the sports day?

b) In a year group with 150 students, 10% passed their English exam. What number of the year group did not pass the English exam?

c) The total cost of the school trip was £350, 10% was charged to the parents. How much does the school contribute? Give your answer in pounds.

d) In a group with 60 pupils, $\frac{1}{4}$ could play an instrument. What number of the group could not play an instrument?

e) New instruments cost 160 pounds, 12.5% of the cost is due to shipping. How much of the cost is not due to shipping?

f) A school fun day cost 480 pounds. $\frac{1}{8}$ of the cost was covered by donations. How much did the school fun day cost after the donations were deducted?

g) In a school with 700 students, 10% passed the annual maths bonanza quiz. How many pupils is this?

h) A school organised a coach to take children to weekly swimming lessons. The coach cost £75 pounds. $\frac{1}{3}$ of the cost was covered by the school. How much did the school pay?

i) In a class of 50 students 10% needed additional support. What number of the class needed additional support?

j) A theme park ticket cost 60 pounds, $\frac{1}{3}$ of this cost was for queue jump. How much of the ticket cost was due to queue jump?

4. Percentage increase and decrease

Introduction

If you can find the percentage of an amount then percentage increase and decrease is very simple. If it is increase you add it on and if it is decrease you take it away. For example, 20 increased by 10% is 22 and 20 decreased by 10% is 18.

Explanation Example

Example 1

Increase 50 by 10%.

1. Find 10%.
2. Increase means add it on.

$$10\% = 50 \div 10 = 5$$
$$50 + 10\% = 50 + 5 = 55$$

Example 2

Decrease 40 by 40%.

1. Find 40%.
2. Decrease means take it away.

$$10\% = 40 \div 10 = 4$$
$$40\% = 10\% \times 4 = 4 \times 4 = 16$$
$$40 - 40\% = 40 - 16 = 24$$

Example 3

Decrease 25 by 5%.

1. Find 5%.
2. Decrease means take it away.

$$10\% = 25 \div 10 = 2.5$$
$$5\% = 10\% \div 2 = 2.5 \div 2 = 1.25$$
$$25 - 5\% = 25 - 1.25 = 23.75$$

Example 4: Test Question

A teacher stretches a **125** millimetre spring *increasing* its size by **75%**. What is the new size of the spring?

$$10\% = 125 \div 10 = 12.5$$
$$70\% = 12.5 \times 7 = 87.5$$
$$5\% = 10\% \div 2 = 12.5 \div 2 = 6.25$$
$$75\% = 87.5 + 6.25 = 93.75$$
$$125 + 93.25 = 218.75mm$$

Example 5: Test Question

A teacher freezes an **80** centimetre elastic band *decreasing* its size by **81%**. What is the new size of the elastic band?

$$10\% = 80 \div 10 = 8$$
$$80\% = 8 \times 8 = 64$$
$$1\% = 10\% \div 10 = 0.8$$
$$81\% = 64 + 0.8 = 64.8$$
$$80 - 64.8 = 15.2 \text{ cm}$$

4.1   I can calculate percentage increase and decrease – TEST Questions

a)   A train operator decreases the price on a £30 return ticket by 5%. How much discount does he give?

b)   A primary school with 100 students increases its capacity by 85%. How many students are now able to attend the primary school?

c)   A drama class of 50 increases in size by 66%. How many people are now in the drama class?

d)   60 teachers attend a union meeting. This number declines by 5% at the next meeting. How many teachers were there at the next union meeting?

e)   A council's school budget increases from 45 million pounds by 90% to enable a region wide school building programme. How much is the council's school budget now?

f) A student breaks a 45-centimetre ruler decreasing its size by 20%. What is the new size of the ruler?

g) A £15 dress in a sale has 25% knocked off its marked price with the use of student discount. What is the new price of the dress?

h) A council estimates that a class of 25 pupils will have increased by 76% in the year 2040. What will be the size of the class in 2040?

i) A trailer contains 120kg of cargo. This is then increased by 35% following a pickup. What is the new weight of the cargo?

j) A teacher runs an after school sports club containing 95 students. The teacher intends to expand the club by increasing the number of places by 60%. How many places are there available in the new class?

5. Conversions (and Ratios)

Introduction

Conversion questions come up in many different scenarios within the skills test. Two common types of conversion questions are based on currency and distance, which is what the test questions in this section will focus on.

To work through the conversion method you need to be comfortable with the fact that equations need to be balanced. By this, we mean, whatever you do to one side of the equation you have to do to the other. Imagine a set of scales with 10kg on one side and five lots of 2kg on the other. The scales are balanced. Provided we perform the same calculation to both sides, such as multiplying by 2, they will remain balanced. Both sides are now 20kg. Equations follow the same rule.

5.1   Conversion Method

Explanation Example

Example 1:

If 5 bananas cost £1, how much will 6 bananas cost?

1. We can work out the cost of one banana by dividing both sides of the equation by 5. This gives us the result of £0.20 or 20p per banana.

2. We then multiply the left hand side by six to give us six bananas.

3. Then we do the same to the right hand side. Six multiplied by 20p is £1.20.

What we know

$$5 \text{ bananas} = £1$$
$$\div 5 \qquad\qquad \div 5$$
$$1 \text{ banana} = £.0.20$$
$$\times 6 \qquad\qquad \times 6$$
$$6 \text{ bananas} = £1.20$$

What we know

Example 2 | Currency | Test Question

The exchange rate is £1 to $1.50. You have £100, how many dollars will you get?

1. Write what we know and what we want.

2. What do we multiply 1 by to get 100?
   $$100 \div 1 = 100$$
3. Multiply both sides by 100.

   $$1.50 \times 100 = 150$$

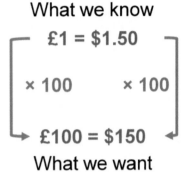

What we know

£1 = $1.50

× 100   × 100

£100 = $150

What we want

Example 3 | Currency | Test Question

The exchange rate is £1 to €0.80. You have £25, how many euros will you get?

1. Write what we know and what we want.
2. What do we multiply by?

   25

3. Multiply both sides by the same.
   $$0.80 \times 25 = 20$$

What we know

£1 = €0.80

× 25   × 25

£25 = €20

What we want

Example 4 | Ratio | Test Question

A sauce has the ingredients butter and flour in the ratio 3:5.
If you measure 150g of flour, how much butter do you need?

1. Write what we know and what we want.

2. We don't know the multiplier.

   The multiplier is 30 (relationship on right).

3. Multiplying the left by 30, 90g butter.

What we know
3 butter : 5 Flour

× 40   × 40

90g butter : 150g Flour

What we want

5.2   I can convert between currencies and distances – TEST Questions

a)   On a trip to the USA, each person received $336. How many pounds did each person exchange assuming £1 pound is equal to $1.4?

b)   A class went to China, each person exchanged 680 pounds. What is this in Yuan assuming £1 is equal to ¥1.3?

c)   During a tour of Asia, the accommodation cost 660 pounds. How many Yuan did the accommodation cost if 1 pound is equal to ¥1.1?

d)   A school went on a trip to France. Knowing 1 pound is equal to 1.2 Euros and each person took 1080 pounds. How many Euros did each person receive?

e)   A class went to Japan, the trip cost 1060 pounds. How many yen did the trip cost each person, if 1 pound is equal to 1.8 yen?

f)   A language class went to Spain. Assuming £1 is equal to €1.4 and the accommodation cost €168, how many pounds did each member of the class have to exchange?

g)   Mrs Smith went on holiday to Sweden. If 1 pound is equal to 1.9 Euros and she spent 722 euros, how many pounds did she spend?

h)   For a tour across China each person swapped £220 to begin with before exchanging an additional £220. How many Yuan did each person swap altogether, given that £1 is equal to ¥1.9?

i)   If 1 pound to 1.7 Euros is the exchange rate, what would a family holiday of four people cost each person if the total holiday cost was 1680 pounds. Give your answer in euros.

j)   1 pound exchanges to 1.1 Euros. Molly and Alice visited their grandparents in Germany, the total amount they exchanged was 520 pounds. How many Euros did they receive?

5.3   I can simplify and divide into ratios

Introduction

Ratio questions are a common feature in the numeracy skills test. You have to be able to work with ratios and simplify them into their lowest form. You can treat ratios in a similar way to conversions, what you do to one side you must do to the other. The following example shows how a ratio is simplified.

Explanation Example

Example 1

Simplify the ratio **3 : 9**.

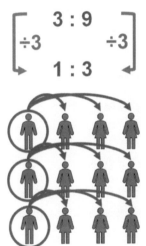

1. What number divides into **3** and **9**?

    3

2. Divide both sides by **3**.

If we had men : women in the ratio **3 : 9** that's the same as 1 man to every three women.

Example 2

Simplify the ratio **33 : 99**.

1. What number divides into **33** and **99**?

    33

2. Divide both sides by **33**.

3. The answer is **1:3**

Example 3

Divide **500** into the ratio **10 : 8 : 7.**

1. How many parts are there in total?

    25

2. How much does one part get?

    20

3. Multiply each part of the ratio by this amount.

$10 : 8 : 7$

$10 + 8 + 7 = 25$

$500 \div 25 = 20$

$10 : 8 : 7$

$\times 20 \ \times 20 \ \times 20$

$200 : 160 : 140$

Example 4: Test Question

A trip is planned for **24 students**. Every **8 students** must be accompanied by **2 adults**. How many **adults** are there on this trip?

In total there are 6 adults

5.4 · I can simplify and divide ratios – TEST Questions

a) In a school there are 48 full time teaching staff. For every 2 full time teachers there is 1 part time teacher or teaching assistant. How many part time teachers and teaching assistants are there in total?

b) For each pupil in a school there are 3 exercise books allocated. If the school requires 450 exercise books, how many pupils are there?

c) In a special needs school, rules state that for every 6 students there must be 2 members of staff. If there are 16 people in total, how many staff members are there?

d)   At the museum, 6 students must be accompanied by 2 adults. If there are 72 students, how many people are there in total?

e)   Every 5 classrooms must have at least 4 fire extinguishers There are 25 classrooms. What is the minimum number of fire extinguishers required?

f)   A booklet project requires 27 white pages to 3 blue pages. If there are 90 pages in total, how many of the pages are blue?

g)   An experiment is planned for 24 students. Every 8 students must be accompanied by 3 demonstrators. How many demonstrators are there for this experiment?

h)   Every 6 students share 2 revision worksheets. If there is 42 students in total how many revision worksheets will there be?

i)   On a school rugby tour, for every 6 students 3 rugby balls are given out to practice with. If there is 48 students in total, how many rugby balls will there be?

j)   For every 18ml of water there must be 2ml of juice. In an 80ml mixture of juice and water, what is the volume of water?

6. Time

Introduction

The problem with time is there is a temptation to assume that you're working with decimal numbers which come in blocks of 10 and 100 rather than blocks of 60. There is a natural temptation to say that 0.25 of an hour is 25 minutes, whereas, 0.25 of an hour is the same as one quarter of an hour, which is 15 minutes.

We recommend making sure you are completely comfortable with your conversions between fractions and decimals, on **page 35**, as these play an important role in the conversion of decimals to minutes.

Explanation Example

Example 1

The game starts at 15:00 and lasts for 105 minutes. At what time does it end?

1. How many whole hours are there in 105 minutes?
2. Work out how many minutes are left over?
3. Add on the hours then the minutes to 15:00.

105 minutes

1 hour = 60

2 hours = 120

Therefore, 1 whole hour (60m).

105 − 60 = 45m

15:00 + 01:00 = 16:00

16:00 + 00:45 = 16:45

The game ends at 16:45

Example 2: Test Question

The event starts at 19:00 and lasts for 215 minutes. At what time does it end?

1. How many whole hours are there in 215 minutes?
2. Work out how many minutes are left over?
3. Add on the hours then the minutes to 19:00.

215 minutes

1 hour = 60

2 hours = 120

3 hours = 180

Therefore, 3 whole hours.

215 − 180 = 35m

19:00 + 03:00 = 22:00

22:00 + 00:35 = 22:35

The event ends at 22:35

Example 3: Test Question

The day starts at 09:00 and lasts for 365 minutes. At what time does it end? Give your answer in am/pm.

1. How many whole hours are there in 365 minutes?
2. Work out how many minutes are left over?
3. Add on the hours then the minutes to 09:00.
4. Convert to pm by taking away 12.

365 minutes

1h = 60, 2h = 120, 3h = 180, 4h= 240, 5h= 300, 6h= 360

Therefore, 6 whole hours.

365 − 360 = 5m

09:00 + 06:00 = 15:00

15:00 + 00:05 = 15:05

15:05 − 12:00 = 03:05pm

The day ends at 3:05pm

Example 4: Test Question

The day starts at 09:00. There are 3 lessons of 50 minutes and 1 break of 15 minutes before lunch. What time does lunch start?

1. How many minutes do we have to add in total?

2. How many hours are in 165 minutes?

3. Work out how many minutes are left over?

4. Add the hours then the minutes to 09:00.

$50 \times 3 = 150$

$150 + 15 = 165$

1h = 60, 2h = 120, 3h = 180

2 whole hours.

$165 - 120 = 45m$

$09:00 + 02:00 = 11:00$

$11:00 + 00:45 = 11:45$

Lunch starts at 11:45.

6.1   I can solve problems that involve time – TEST Questions

a)   A presentation ends at 11.15am after lasting for 55 minutes. This is followed by 3 speeches each lasting 55 minutes. At what time does the day finish?

b)   Two students both submit an art project. One student spends 5 hours and 25 minutes on the project whilst the other spends 2 hours and 50 minutes. What is the difference between the students in the time spent completing the project?

c)   A student union meeting starts at 10.00am and lasts for 30 minutes. Due to unforeseen circumstances the meeting overruns by 2 minutes. This is followed by 2 additional meetings each lasting 50 minutes. At what time does the day end?

d)   A student helpline is open for 5 hours 50 minutes on a Saturday, Tuesday, Thursday and Wednesday and 6 hours 40 minutes on a Sunday and Friday. In total, for how many hours does the helpline open?

e)   A sports event starts at 11.30am and lasts for 25 minutes. This is followed by 5 training sessions each lasting 40 minutes. At what time does the sports event finish?

f)   A welcome session ends at 4.30pm after lasting for 35 minutes. This is following 2 information sessions each lasting 5 minutes. At what time does the day start?

g)   The computer backup system runs for 3 hours 50 minutes on a Saturday and Thursday and 5 hours 40 minutes on a Tuesday, Friday and Monday. In one week, how many hours and minutes is this?

h)   In a typical week a reception is staffed for 3 hours 30 minutes on a Monday and Tuesday and 5 hours a day for the remaining weekdays. How many hours is the reception staffed in a typical week?

i)   A student library opens for 2 hours 10 minutes on a Monday and 7 hours 20 minutes for the rest of the days of the week except Sunday when it is closed. How long does the library open for each week? Give your answer in hours and minutes.

j)   A student helpdesk opens for 6 hours 20 minutes for 3 days a week. In any given week, how many hours does the helpdesk open?

60
120
180
240

7. Shapes

Introduction

More shape questions have started appearing in the skills test since 2018. These questions include area, perimeter and volume and they rely on the arithmetic skills you have practised earlier on in this book.

Explanation Example

Example 1

Calculate the perimeter and area of a rectangle with length 4cm and width 3cm.

1. The perimeter is the distance around the outside. This can also be calculated by 2 times the length plus 2 times the width.

2. The area is the number of 1cm² blocks there are inside. This can be calculated by multiplying the length by the width.

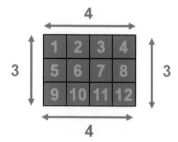

Perimeter = 4 + 3 + 4 + 3
= 14cm

Perimeter = (2 × 4) + (2 × 3) =
14cm

Area = 12cm²

Units for area are always squared

Area = 4 × 3 = 12cm²

Example 2

Calculate the perimeter and area of a rectangle with length 8cm and width 2cm.

1. The perimeter is calculated by 2 times the length plus 2 times the width.

2. The area is calculated by multiplying the length by the width.

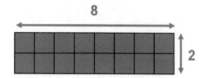

Perimeter = (2 × 8) + (2 × 2) =
16 + 4 = 20cm

Area = 8 × 2 = 16cm²

Units for area are always squared

Example 3

Calculate the volume of a cuboid with length 4cm, width 2cm and depth 3cm.

Method 1

We can also calculate the volume by multiplying the width, length and depth together.

$$2 \times 4 \times 3 = 24 \; cm^3$$

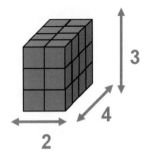

Volume = 24 cm³

Units for volume are always cubed

Example 4: Test Question

A large train station building has a width of **80m**, a length of **450m** and a ceiling height of **5m**. What is the volume of the train station building?

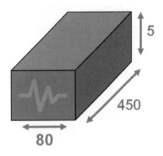

V= 80 × 5 × 450 = 400 × 450

×	400	50	
400	160,000	20,000	180,000

Volume = 180,000 m³

7.1   I can calculate perimeter, area and volume – TEST Questions

a) A book in a library has a width of 35 cm and a length of 40 cm. Calculate its perimeter.

b) A shredder in the schools admin office measures 160 cm by 500 cm by 70 cm. What is the volume of the shredder?

c) A poster for the wall has a width of 80 cm and a length of 120 cm. What is the area of the poster?

d) Four tables are positioned adjacent to each other, forming a single shape. Each table measures 75 cm by 100 cm. What is the area of one table?

e) Two rooms in a school have their carpet tiles replaced. Each room has a width of 40 m and a length of 40 m. What is the total area of floor that needs carpet tiles replacing?

f) A plastic tub has a width of 160 cm, a length of 300 cm and a depth of 80 cm. What is the volume of the plastic tub?

g) A packing box at a school measures 70 cm by 300 cm by 100 cm. What is the volume of the packing box?

h) What is the area of a playing field which has a width of 65 m and a length of 290 m?

i) A packing box at a primary school measures 40 cm by 450 cm by 40 cm. What is the volume of the packing box?

j) A playing field at a school has a width of 70 m and a length of 220 m. What is the perimeter of the field?

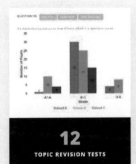

Written Data Section (Calculator Allowed)

In the written data part of the exam you will come across many different question types that look to present data in various formats. You are permitted to use a calculator in the second part of the test which is composed of 16 questions, most of which require multiple calculations.

QTS Maths Tutor has created an online calculator which mimics the calculator that you have to use in the real exam. It does take a while to get comfortable using the calculator so we recommend that you practise using it. You can access the calculator at: www.QTSmathstutor.co.uk/calculator/

The methods and techniques learnt in the mental arithmetic part of this book will help you to determine what calculations you need to make in order to get to the right answer; however there are also a lot of additional skills to learn such as how to read box plots and cumulative frequency curves amongst other things.

In this part of the book each area of the written data section of the numeracy skills test will be covered with explanations and examples to help you revise effectively. To practise questions in the onscreen exam format like the actual test we recommend you visit the QTS Maths Tutor website.

8. Using the Calculator

This section covers many of the topics covered in the mental arithmetic section. However this time you will have the aid of a calculator. As a result of this the emphasis is shifted away from your ability to perform the calculation, and onto your ability to spot which type of calculation you need to perform, whether it be multiplication, division, etc.

We recommend you refresh yourself on Section 1 Multiplication on **page 12**, section 2 Division on **page 25** and Section 5 Conversions on **page 46** before continuing.

8.1   I can perform multiplication using a calculator

Explanation Example

Each year Birdholme Avenue Academy buy 9600 workbooks, which cost £0.01 per page. Each book contains 90 pages. 1000 books can fit in one box; each box comes with a shipping charge of £4.95. How much will the total bill be?

First we need to calculate the total number of pages in all 9600 books.

$$9600 \times 90 = 864000 \text{ pages}$$

Next we need to calculate the cost for all these pages.

$$864000 \times £0.01 = £8640$$

Finally we need to add on the postage. The question says it is £4.95 for each 1000 books posted. We have 9600 books so this will mean we need 10 boxes.

$$10 \times £4.95 = £49.5$$

Adding the shipping and book costs together gives the final answer:

$$£49.5 + £8640 = £8689.50$$

8.2   I can perform multiplication using a calculator – TEST questions

a)   A teacher plans a school trip, which includes 8 adults and 22 children. Each person going on the trip must pay £87 for food and accommodation and an additional cost for entrance to the museum. Adults are charged at £7.95 and children at £4.95. What is the total cost of the trip?

b)   A head teacher must travel from School A to School B which are a distance of 14 miles apart then onto School C which is a further 17 miles. The trip back home is then another 28 miles. She can claim back 40p per mile for the trips between the schools but not her journey back home. Each mile she travels in her car costs her 14p. How much money will she have in total once her costs and claims have been accounted for?

c)   Johnny gets two buses to school each day, the first bus costs him £2.40 and the second is £1.90. He makes the journey 195 times a year, how much does this cost him in total?

d)   A teaching conference is to be held in Beijing. The outbound and return flight costs are shown in the table below. How much does Mrs Swift save by choosing to fly Option 1 in comparison to option 3.

Option 1	London	497.96	Doha	659.21	Beijing
Option 2	London	499	Abu Dhabi	729.49	Beijing
Option 3	London	499.98	Abu Dhabi	719.49	Beijing

e) The school party needs 121 cartons of orange juice, 56 bags of crisps, 16 loaves of bread and 12 bags of sweets. In total how much will this cost?

Item	Price
Cartons of Orange Juice (Pack of 11)	£2.99
Crips (Pack of 8)	£1.80
Bread (Per loaf)	£0.40
Sweets (Pack of 12)	£6.95

f) There are 124 children going on a school trip, the tickets cost £17.95 each. If the bill is greater than £2000, there is a 15% discount. How much is the total cost including the discount (if required)?

g) Mr Jennings performs a sponsored 1200-mile cycle over summer. Three teachers sponsor him, the details of which are below.

Miss Telford "50p per mile for the first 1000 miles, then 75p for each mile after."

Mr Hawkins "60p per mile."

Dr Granger "£1.20 per mile for the first 500, £1.00 per mile for the next 500 and 50p per mile for the next 200."

Work out the total amount of money raised.

8.3   I can perform division using a calculator

Explanation Example

Lucy must decide at the start of the year whether to buy daily, monthly or yearly bus tickets.

	Cost per ticket (£)	Has to buy	Total cost
Daily	2	195	390
Month	35	11	385
Yearly	400	1	400

Work out the cost per day, assuming she uses the bus 195 days per year and establish which ticket works out the best value for money?

From the table we can see that daily tickets cost £2 per day.
Second, monthly tickets

1. We need to calculate the cost per year

$$£35 \times 11 = £385$$

2. Then we need to divide by the number of days to find the cost per day.

$$£385 \div 195 = £1.97 \text{ per day}$$

Thirdly, yearly tickets

We know the tickets cost £400 per year. So to find the cost per day we need to divide £400 by the number of days.

$$£400 \div 195 = £2.05 \text{ per day}$$

From this we can see that the **monthly** tickets are the cheapest.

8.4   I can perform division using a calculator – TEST questions

a) Thirty Mereside School pupils went on a hiking trip. The total cost was £188.50. The bus cost £100 and the rest was spent on lunches. How much did each lunch cost?

b) Mrs Cauldy, the caretaker, travels a total of 50.75 miles in a week. This is made up of journeys to and from school, which is 3.625 miles away from her home. How many times did she perform the return journey that week?

c) The annual electricity bill for a school is £179400. This is based on lights and appliances being used for 8 hours per day, 195 days a year. How much does 1 hour of electricity cost the school on average?

d) Use the table below to work out who earned the most stars per day?

	Days at School	Stars Earned
Alfie	195	92
Beatrice	172	87
Calum	190	83
Della	192	90
Emily	189	46
Fran	180	86

e) If there are 39 weeks in a school year and 195 teaching days, what is the average number of teaching days per teaching week?

f) Seven boys and eight girls each order a new PE kit, consisting of a shirt and shorts. The total bill is £225. The shirts cost £9 each, how much do the shorts cost?

g) In total, the 402 pupils at Clifford Primary used 8522.4m² of paper in one year. Assuming they all used the same amount, how much did one pupil use?

8.5   I can perform compound conversions

Explanation Example

A car with a flat tyre is travelling at 98.4 meters per minute. You may assume 1 mile is 1610 meters. What is the speed of the car in miles per hour? Give your answer to two decimal places.

First let's convert meters into miles.

To do this we need to divide the number of meters we have, by how many meters go into a mile, in this case 1610.

(Tip: to check you are doing it correctly you can use your knowledge that a mile is larger than a meter. So when converting from meters to miles your answer needs to be getting smaller)

$$98.4 \div 1610 = 0.06111801242 \text{ miles per minute}$$

Next we need to convert from minutes to hours. To do this we need to multiply by 60.

(Tip: To check you are doing it correctly, remember you will travel a greater distance in an hour than in a minute, so your answer needs to be getting bigger.)

$$0.061 \times 60 = 3.6671 \text{ miles per hour}$$

Finally, we need to round to 2 decimal places.

This gives an answer of 3.67 mph.

8.6   I can perform compound conversions - TEST questions

To revise conversions please see the conversion method on **page 46.**

a)   Fuel was purchased at a cost of 1.20€ per litre. Knowing that 4.546 litres = 1 gallon and that £1 = 1.30€, how much is the cost in £ per gallon. Give your answer to the nearest penny.

b)   Bryony completes the LRO Marathon in the USA. She averages a speed of 9 miles per hour. Using 1 mile = 8/5 km and 1 minute = 1/60 hour work out her time in km per minute.

c)   A car is travelling at 13.4m/s. What is this in miles per hour? You may assume 1 mile is 1610 metres. Give your answer to two decimals places.

d)   The bamboo plant in Dr Klein's garden is a type that under the optimum conditions can grow up to 40m a year. Assuming one day is precisely 24 hours, calculate the rate of growth in mm per hour. Give your answer to 2 decimal places. (Use 1 year as exactly 365 days)

e)   A sponsored cycle across Spain covers a distance of 500km. Each km was sponsored at 1€ per km. 5M = 8KM. 1€ = £0.75. The total amount raised was £575. What was the sponsorship rate in €s per mile? Give your answer to the nearest whole cent.

f)   Mrs Barrington has a textbook in which the density of gold is given as 0.698 pounds per cubic inch. Taking one cubic inch as 16.39 cubic centimetre and 1 pound as 453.59 grams, convert the density of gold into grams per cubic centimetre, giving your answer to one decimal place.

g)   A trip around Spain covers a distance of 790km. The fuel for this trip cost 1.30€ per litre. Knowing that 4.546 litres = 1 gallon and that £1 is 1.05€, how much is the cost of the fuel in pounds per gallon.

9. Averages

Introduction

Averages is the all-encompassing term which describes not only the mean (add them all up, divide by how many there are) but also the mode (most common), the median (the one in the middle) and sometimes the range (difference between largest and smallest value). The questions referring to averages in the skills test use tables or graphs to represent the data.

9.1   Calculating Mean, Mode, Median and Range

Explanation Example

On a school sports day 16 girls throw a shot, the distances are recorded to the nearest metre and displayed in the table below.

Distance (m)	Frequency (F)
1	2
2	3
3	7
4	4

Example 1: How to calculate the mean

Calculate the **mean** distance of the shots thrown to the nearest cm?

When in a frequency table we need to multiply the frequency by the units, in this case distance thrown. The table below shows that 2 people threw the shot put 1 m, 3 threw the shot put 2 m and so on.

We then add up the total distance thrown by all students, then divide by the number of students.

Distance (m)	Frequency (F)	D × F
1	2	1 × 2 = 2
2	3	2 × 3 = 6
3	7	3 × 7 = 21
4	4	4 × 4 = 16
		Sum = 45

Mean = 45 ÷ 16 = **2.81m**

Example 2: How to calculate the median

On a schools sports day 16 girls throw a shot, the distance is recorded to the nearest m. Workout the median distance the shot was thrown to the nearest cm?

Median – the one in the middle.

Using the rule:

$$Put\ the\ set\ in\ ascending\ order\ then\ find\ the\ \frac{n+1}{2}^{th}\ term$$

Median = (16 + 1) ÷ 2 = **8.5th distance**

Distance (m)	Frequency (F)	Running total number of people
1	2	2
2	3	+ 5
3	7	←8.5 distance + 12
4	4	+ 16

Median distance = **3m**

Example 3: How to find the mode and range

On a school sports day 16 girls throw a shot, the distance is recorded to the nearest m. Workout the mode and range of the distances to the nearest cm?

Mode – the one that appears the most.

Range – maximum value subtract the minimum.

Distance (D)	Frequency (F)
1	2
2	3
3	7
4	4

Mode = **3m**
(7 people achieved this)

Range = 4m – 1m = **3m**

n work out the mean, median, mode and range – SKILLS questions.

..... out the mean, median, mode and range of each of the following:

a) 2, 4, 4, 1, 4

g) 18, 47, 41, 14, 5, 29, 44

b) 6, 5, 4, 6, 6

h) 0, 1, 1, 0, 1, 0, 1

c) 5, 4, 2, 1, 7, 7

i) 2.1, 3.1, 4.2, 3.2, 3.3

d) 10, 12, 7, 6, 85, 21

j) 0.8, 0.3, 0, 0.5

e) 23, 53, 19, 17, 11, 103

k) 0.1, 0.3, 0.6, 0, 0.9

f) 46, 43, 2, 6

l) 0.5, 0.8, 0.7, 0.5, 0.8, 0.7, 0.5

For each of the following frequency tables work out the mean, median, mode and range:

m)

Amount (£)	Frequency
0.50	1
1.00	2
1.50	3
2.00	2
2.50	1

n)

Amount (£)	Frequency
5.00	4
10.00	4
15.00	6
20.00	3
25.00	2

o)

Amount (£)	Frequency
1.00	7
2.00	11
3.00	15
4.00	16
5.00	14

P)

Sweets	Frequency
1	6
2	4
3	5
4	1
5	7

9.3   I can work out the mean, median, mode and range – TEST questions

a) A teacher recorded the volume of water drank by each of her pupils, as shown in the table below.

Girls		Boys	
Water Drank (ml)	Number of Pupils	Water Drank (ml)	Number of Pupils
400	5	400	6
500	5	500	10
600	7	600	6
700	5	700	2
800	2	800	7

(handwritten annotations: girls — 11, 15, 17, 22, 24; boys — 13, 7, 9, 31)

Select all **TRUE** statements from the list below:

i)   The mean volume drank by the girls was more than the boys.

ii)   More boys than girls drank 700ml of water or more.

iii) Twice as many girls than boys drank 400ml.

iv) There are more boys than girls.

v)   The median girl drank 600ml of water.

vi) The median boy drank 600ml of water.

vii) One third of the pupils who drank 500ml were girls.

viii) The mode value drank by girls and boys was 500ml.

ix) One eighth of the pupils who drank 800ml were girls.

x)   The range of water drank for both sets of pupils is 400ml.

xi) There are at least 20% more boys than girls.

xii) The mean amount drank by girls is 575ml.

b) A teacher summarised the 90 science test grades of his pupils, as shown in the table below (each of the 30 pupils took three tests).

GCSE Grade	Biology	Chemistry	Physics
9	1	4	0
8	1	3	2
7	5	4	3
6	7	4	9
5	4	5	6
4	3	4	4
3	3	3	4
2	4	2	2
1	2	1 30·	0 30

Select all **TRUE** statements from the list below:

i)	The range of grades for all three papers is the same.
ii)	Chemistry has the highest mean grade of the three papers.
iii)	The median grade for biology is 5.
iv)	The lowest grade achieved in physics is Grade 1.
v)	The mean grade for biology is less than 5.
vi)	The median grade for physics is 5.
vii)	Of the 90 grades achieved across the three papers, 1/6 were for grade 3.
viii)	The median grade for chemistry is 5.
ix)	Over 1/3 of pupils achieved a grade 7 or higher in chemistry.
x)	The modal grade for biology is grade 6.
xi)	The mean grade for physics is 5.2
xii)	One sixth of the biology grades are Grade 7.

9.4   Potential values

Potential values is a subtopic of averages. These questions are usually quite tricky and therefore it is good to get plenty of practice. They require you to determine certain facts based on your knowledge of averages and the data presented. We recommend that you become confident with the types of averages and their definitions, which can be revised on **page 69**, before continuing.

Explanation Example

A summary table of French test marks for Class A and Class B is displayed in the table below.

Class	Median	Mode	Range
A	73	65	21
B	69	62	33

We know certain facts about averages, for instance all values must be within the range. We know some values (in this instance the median and mode) and using these we can estimate the limits of the rest of the data.

a) At least one person scored 90 in test A, True or False?

We need to use the lowest mark we know someone achieved in test A, this would be the mode mark 65. We also know the range of marks. From this we can draw the following diagram.

Write out values you know – median and mode.

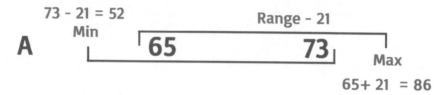

$73 - 21 = 52$

Min

A 65   73

Range - 21

Max

$65+ 21 = 86$

Adding the range of marks to the lowest mark gives us the highest possible mark. And subtracting the range from the highest mark gives us the lowest possible mark given the information we have.

From this we can see the highest possible mark is 86, and the lowest possible mark is 52. We can therefore say this statement is FALSE. It is not possible for anybody to have scored 90.

b) The lowest mark achieved in Class B was 32, True or False?

We can see that the highest mark we know of is the median which is 69. We know the range of marks is 33. From this we can draw the following diagram.

$69 - 33 = 36$

Min

B 62   69

Range - 33

Max

$62 + 33 = 95$

Subtracting the range from the highest mark we know gives us the lowest possible mark given the information we have.

$$69 – 33 = 36$$

Thus, the statement is FALSE; the lowest mark in class B was 36.

9.5 I can work out potential values using a summary table – TEST questions

a) The head of history at Malcolm-Grange summarised the scores the four Year 10 classes got in their tests.

	Marks (Percentage)		
Class	Median	Mode	Range
History A	65	60	32
History B	51	55	49
History C	80	79	5
History D	43	45	16

Select all **TRUE** statements from the list below:

i) From the four classes, the highest possible score anyone achieved was 100%.

ii) All pupils in history C achieved at least 70%.

iii) No one in history A could have scored less than 35.

iv) At least one pupil in history D achieved a score of 45.

v) All pupils in history C achieved at least 75%.

vi) At least one pupil in history B, could have achieved a score of 52.

vii) In class D over half the pupils achieved a score of 50% or more.

viii) The class with the smallest range had the highest median.

ix) The lowest possible mark anyone achieved was 6.

x) Everyone in history C scored less than 80%.

xi) Across the four classes at least half of the pupils achieved 50%.

xii) The most common score in history A was 65.

b) A council recorded the attendance rates of the three primary schools.

	Attendance (Percentage)			
School	Mean	Median	Mode	Range
Almgate	90	91	91	12
Bullroad	94	85	90	14
Carmington	82	91	85	23

Select all **TRUE** statements from the list below:

i)   All of Almgate's students had an attendance above 88%.

ii)   At least one pupil at Bullroad had an attendance of 75%.

iii)   The most common attendance at Almgate was 91%.

iv)   The highest attendance achieved at Almgate was 102%.

v)   The highest attendance achieved at Bullroad was 99%.

vi)   More than 50% of all pupils had attendance over 90%.

vii)   One in two pupils at Almgate has attendance less than 90%.

viii)   It is possible for at least one pupil in Carmington to have an attendance of 68%.

ix)   The most common (in terms of attendance) at Bullroad was absent for every 1 in 10 days.

x)   The mean at Almgate is the lowest possible attendance.

xi)   No pupils as Bullroad had an attendance of less than 80%.

xii)   No pupil at Carmington had an attendance less than 65%.

10. Data Representation

There are many ways in which data can be presented from box plots to two way tables. It is important that you practise each different question type and get used to interpreting the data that is provided. You need to learn what each chart and graph shows and what information you can derive from it. These questions make up a significant proportion of the written data section so please spend the time reading through the examples and method notes.

10.1   I can make inferences using a box plot

Introduction

Box plots are a simple way of representing the median, range and the quartiles of a data set. They are sometimes shown in pairs so that you can easily compare one data set to another.

Explanation Example

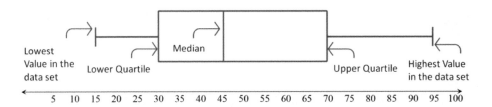

The **median** is the data value in the middle, the person 50% of the way through the sample, the one halfway through. There are two quartiles, first is 25% (1/4) of the way through the data which is called the **lower quartile** and then 75% (3/4) of the way through, which is called the **upper quartile**. All three can be seen in the diagram above.

Calculating the range:

The range can be calculated by doing the following:

Highest value in the data set – Lowest value in the data set

Calculating the interquartile range:

The interquartile range can be calculated by doing the following:

Upper Quartile – Lower Quartile

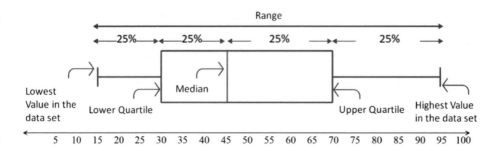

Using the box plot above shows the test scores of 100 students, use this to answer the following example questions:

Example 1: Calculate the median

From the diagram we can see the median is 45 Marks

Example 2: Find the number of students who achieved over 70 marks.

Form the diagram we can see that each section represents 25% of the students.

We can also see that 70 marks lies on the upper quartile, which means that 25% of the students achieved over this score. There are 80 students in total, so 25% of the students equals 20.

Therefore the answer is **20 Students**

Example 3 and 4: The box plots below show people's scores in music and drama tests.

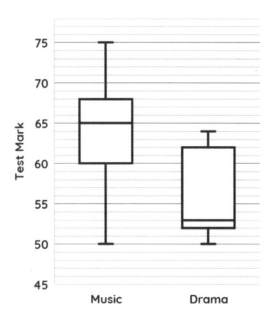

Test Question: Calculate the interquartile range of music marks.

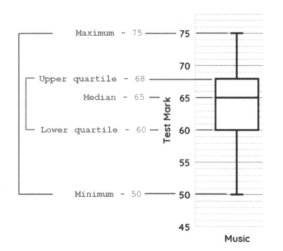

Looking at the box plot for music we can identify all the key features.

We can see the upper quartile is 68 marks and the lower quartile is 60 marks.

We can calculate the interquartile range with the following:

68 – 60 = 8 marks

Test Question: Calculate the range of drama marks.

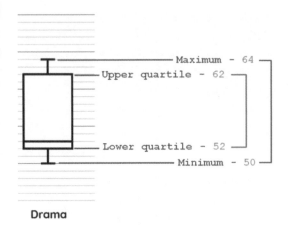

Maximum - 64
Upper quartile - 62
Lower quartile - 52
Minimum - 50

Drama

Looking at the box plot for drama we can identify all the key features.

We can see the highest mark is 64 and the lowest mark is 50.

We can calculate the range with the following:

$$64 - 50 = 14 \text{ marks}$$

10.2   I can make inferences using a box plot – TEST questions

a) A comparison of absence for Years 4 and 5 is conducted using the box plots below.

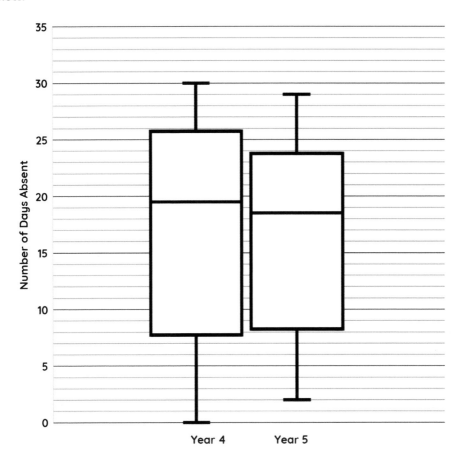

Select all **FALSE** statements from the list below:

i)   No one in Year 5 had 0 days absent.

ii)   The median for Year 4 is 19.5 days.

iii)   The range of days for Year 4 is greater than that of Year 5.

iv)   The maximum number of days absent was 26.

v)   At least one pupil had no days absent.

vi)   In Year 5, the maximum number of days absent was 29.

vii)   Over 50% of Year 4 had at least 20 days absent.

viii) The interquartile range is larger in Year 4 than Year 5.

ix) Someone was absent for 32 days.

x) In Year 5, the minimum number of days absent was 2.

xi) In Year 4, at least one person had 30 days absent.

xii) The median number of days is greater in Year 4 than Year 5.

b) Mr Peek compares the Mathematics test results of Class A to Class B

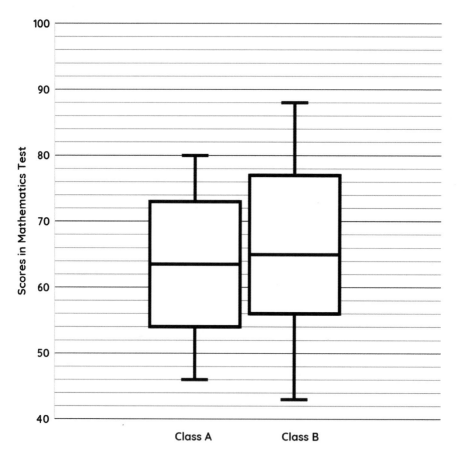

Select all **FALSE** statements from the list below:

i)   The upper quartile for Class A is 73.

ii) Class B has a larger range of scores than Class A.

iii) The lower quartile for Class A is 59.

iv) The highest mark scored was from Class A.

v)   The median score of Class B is 65.

vi) The median score of Class A is 64.

vii) The range of marks for Class A is 34.

viii) Over 50% of Class B scored less than 56 marks.

ix) The upper quartile for Class B is 77.

x)   The interquartile range of Class A is 31.

xi) At least one person scored 88.

xii) More people in Class B achieved a higher mark than those in Class A.

10.3 I can make inferences using a scatter graph

Introduction

Scatter graphs are a way of representing two bits of data relating to one item or person. For example, one person's scores in two exams, or one car's distance travelled and the amount of petrol used. Take a look at the example scatter graph below:

Explanation Example

The graph below shows three people's scores in an English and Mathematics test.

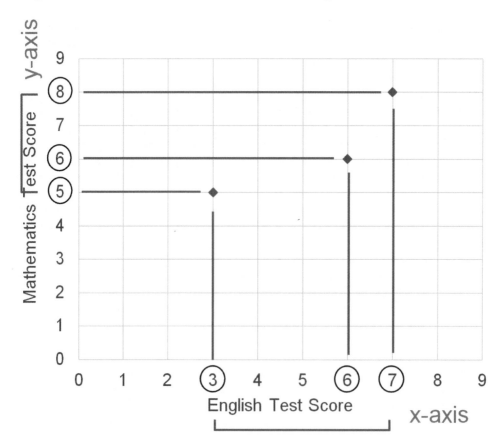

What this graph shows:

This graph shows three students

- Student 1: 7 in English, 8 in maths
- Student 2: 6 in English, 6 in maths
- Student 3: 3 in English, 5 in maths

Calculating the range:

To calculate the range we subtract the lowest score from the highest:

- Range of maths scores 8 − 5 = 3
- Range of English scores 7 − 3 = 4

Calculating the mean:

We need to add up the scores then divide by how many there are.

- Mean maths = (8 + 6 + 5) ÷ 3 = 6.33
- Mean English = (7 + 6 + 3) ÷ 3 = 5.33

Finding the median

We need to find the middle value:

- 6 is the Median maths score
- 6 is the Median English score

Example Test Question 1: At least one student scored an 8 in the mathematics test, True or False?

We can see that student 1 scored a 7 in English and 8 in maths. Thus this statement is **TRUE.**

Example Test Question 2: Two students scored a level 6 in the English test, True or False?

We can see the English scores are 3, 6, and 7. Therefore this statement is **FALSE.**

10.4 I can make inferences using a scatter graph – TEST questions

a) Below the results of a maths and English test are displayed for students of one specific class.

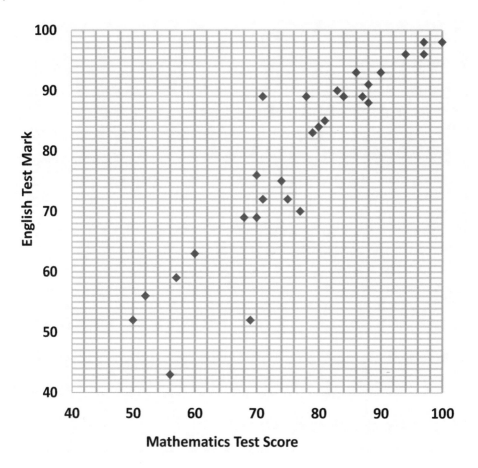

Select all **TRUE** statements from the list below:

i)	The lowest mark in the English test was 43.
ii)	Forty people took both tests.
iii)	More people scored a higher mark in English than in maths.
iv)	The person who scored 56 in mathematics scored 44 in English.
v)	The highest English mark was 98.
vi)	Two pupils scored 98 in English.

vii)	One person scored 89 in English.
viii)	The person that achieved a mark of 50 in mathematics also achieved a mark of 50 in English.
ix)	The highest mark in mathematics was 98.
x)	A person who achieved 70 in English would be expected to achieve 70 in mathematics
xi)	Ten people scored less than 70 in mathematics.
xii)	One person scored the same in English and mathematics.

b) A school offers French revision lessons before registration to see if this helps to improve test marks. Below shows the marks in a French test and school journey time for a group of students. Longer journey times generally resulted in less time in the French revision class.

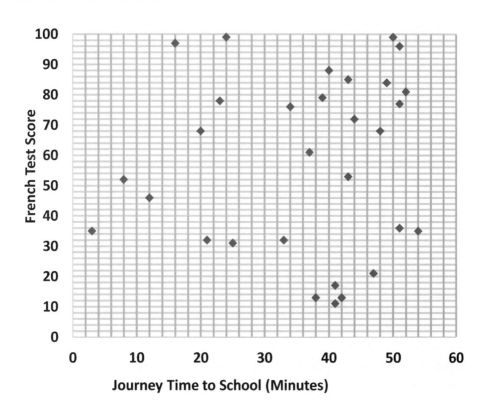

Select all **TRUE** statements from the list below:

i)   No journey to school took longer than 60 minutes.

ii) Only three people scored less than 20 marks in the French test.

iii) The pupil who took 54 minutes to get to school achieved fewer than 40 marks in the French test.

iv) No one who took more than 30 minutes to get to school achieved a mark above 50.

v)   At least one pupil achieved 99 on their French test.

vi) The range of journey times was 51 minutes.

vii) Seven people scored less than 10 marks in the French test.

viii) The median journey time to school was 30 minutes.

ix) The range in French Test marks was 90.

x)   Brian achieved a mark of 35, which means his journey to school was 3 minutes.

xi) No journey to school was shorter than 5 minutes.

xii) Five people scored between 70 and 80 in the French test.

10.5 I can make inferences using a line graph

Introduction

Line graphs are similar to scatter plots in their lay out but the points on the graph are joined up. They are commonly used to show how something changes over time. The idea being you have points that you join up with a line which shows you the general trend of the data and also enables you to estimate values between the data points by using the line.

Explanation Example

The graph below shows the temperature of two locations in a school over the spring term.

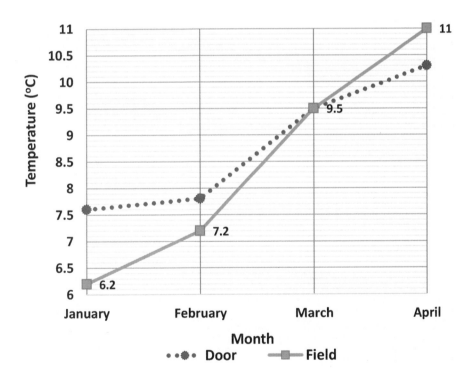

Find the range of temperatures:

To calculate the range we subtract the lowest temperature from the highest:

- Door Temp. range = 10.3 − 7.6 = 2.7
- Field Temp. range = 11 − 6.2 = 4.8

Calculating the mean:

We need to add up the temperatures then divide by the number of readings:

- Door mean = (10.3 + 9.5 +7.8 +7.6) ÷ 4 = 8.8
- Field mean = (11 + 9.5 +7.2 + 6.2) ÷ 4 = 8.475

Example Question: Calculate the percentage temperature increase for the field from February to March. Give your answer to 2 decimal places.

To calculate percentage increase we need to use the equation (found in the help sheet)

$$Percentage\ increase = \left(\frac{Increase}{Original}\right) \times 100$$

Temperature in February = 7.2 °C

Temperature in March = 9.5 °C

Temperature increase = 9.5 - 7.2 = 2.3 °C

We can then insert these figures to the equation above, which gives:

$$\left(\frac{2.3}{7.2}\right) \times 100 = 31.944444 = 31.94$$

This the percentage increases as **31.94 %** *(2 d.p.)*

10.6   I can make inferences using a line graph – TEST questions

a) The average reading age of pupils at a school is compared to the regional average.

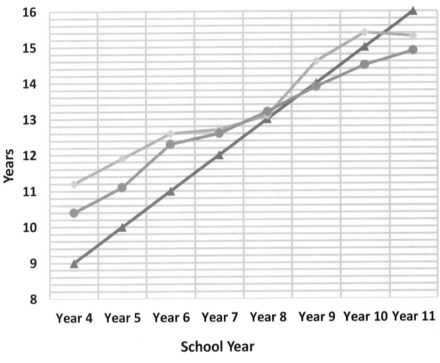

Years / School Year

—▲—Actual Age   —◇—School Reading Age   —●—Regional Reading Age

Select all **FALSE** statements from the list below:

i)   The school average was greater than the actual age for all but one school year.

ii)   There was less than one year between the school average and regional average for the Year 4.

iii)   The range of reading ages for the region was 4 years.

iv)   In total 8 school years are represented on the graph.

v)   The school's Year 7's had an average reading age of 12.

vi) From Year 8 to Year 11, the region had a higher reading age than the school.

vii) The regional average reading age was more than one year below their actual age for Year 11.

viii) The actual age of Year 4's is 9.

ix) The median school reading age is 12.9.

x) The regional average reading age for Year 11 was 14.2.

xi) The median regional reading age is 12.9 years.

xii) The maximum school reading age was 15.1.

b) The temperatures at two locations throughout the year at Brookhill School are displayed below.

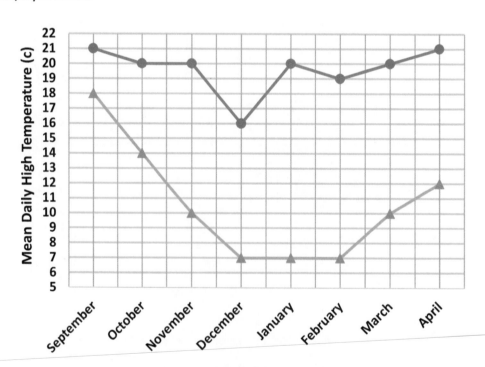

School Year

— Reception   — School Field

Select all **TRUE** statements from the list below

  i)   The school field was warmer than reception for 2 months.

  ii)   The maximum temperature was 21 degrees.

  iii) The lowest reception temperature was in December.

  iv)   The range of temperatures on the school field was 10.

  v)   April was cooler than March in reception.

  vi)   January was colder than February on the field.

  vii) The school field was 9 degrees in November.

  viii) The school field was 20 degrees in April.

  ix)   In March, reception was 20 degrees.

  x)   In March the field was 12 degrees.

  xi)   The median school field temperature was 12 degrees.

  xii) The range of temperatures in reception was 5 degrees.

10.7   I can make inferences using a bar chart

Introduction

Bar charts are another way of viewing a single data set or comparing multiple data sets. They are amongst the simplest forms of representing data but there are a few variations that you need to familiarise yourself with. These are covered in the following examples.

Explanation Example

The graph below shows Year 3 pet ownership split into what the boys own and what the girls own. The person who summarised the data stacked the values of dog, cat and other pet ownership on top of each other. This is often how they appear in the actual exam questions.

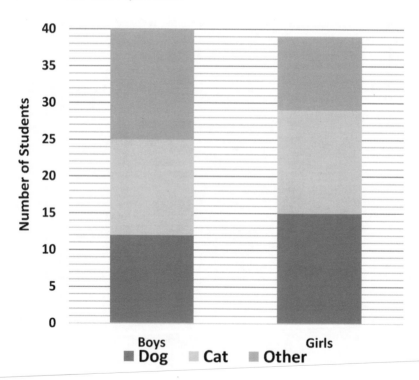

Example Question 1: Calculate how many boys had dogs, cats and others pets.

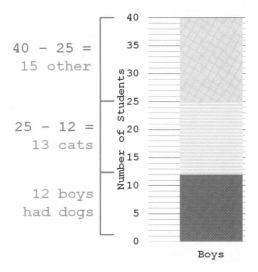

40 – 25 =
    15 other

25 – 12 =
    13 cats

12 boys
had dogs

By looking at the key we can see the top section shows others, middle section is cats, and the bottom section is dogs.

We then need to look at the height of each section independently to find out how many are in each section.

From this we can work out that the boys owned 12 dogs, 13 cats and 15 other pets.

Example Question 2: Calculate the percentage of girls who own dogs. Give your answer to 2 decimal places.

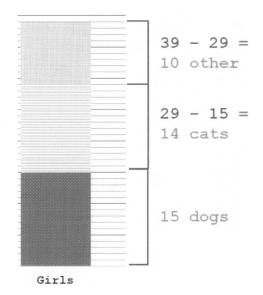

39 – 29 =
10 other

29 – 15 =
14 cats

15 dogs

First we have to calculate how many girls have each pet in the same way as the previous example. From this we can work out that the girls owned 15 dogs, 14 cats and 10 other pets.

Next we need to work out the percentage of dogs owned by girls compared to the total number of pets owned by girls.

To do this we calculate:

$$\left(\frac{15}{39}\right) \times 100 = 38.461..$$

$$= 38.46\,\%$$

10.8 I can make inferences using a bar chart – TEST questions

a) The graph below shows the year-on-year change of those who received the equivalent of 5 A*-C grade GCSEs at Sectorwold School.

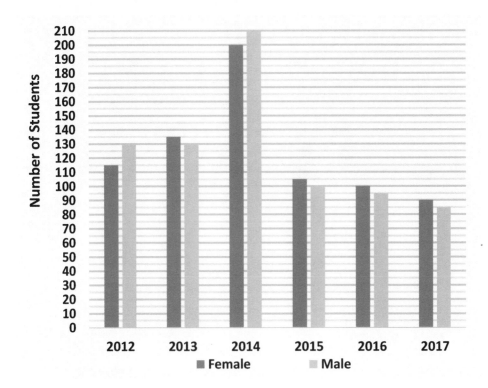

Select all **TRUE** statements from the list below

i)	The year 2017 saw the lowest number of passes for both males and females.
ii)	The number of females who passed increased between 2012 and 2013.
iii)	The number of female passes increased by over 50% from 2013 to 2014.
iv)	Only 85 males passed in 2017.
v)	Across the six years the median number of boys who passed is 110.
vi)	The number of female passes increases every year.
vii)	311 males passed in the years 2015, 2016 and 2017.

viii) Across the six years the median number of boys who passed is 124.

ix) The range of number passes each year for females is 110.

x) From 2016 to 2017 the number of passes dropped by 20%.

xi) The range of number passes each year for males is 115.

xii) Across the six years, 855 females passed.

b) The teachers at Rother Junior School asked the pupils in each year their preferred sport. The results are represented below in a stacked bar chart.

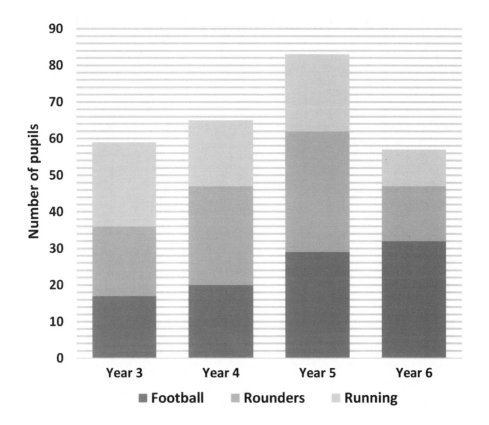

Select all **FALSE** statements from the list below

i) More Year 3s preferred running to rounders.

ii) The most popular sport in the school was rounders.

iii) More children in Year 4 preferred running to those in Year 5.

iv) The median number of children who preferred rounders is 23.

v) 21 Year 4s chose football as their favourite sport.

vi) The number who preferred running decreased with each school year.

vii) There are 60 children in Year 3.

viii) 18 children in Year 4 chose running as their favourite sport.

ix) There were 94 children in the school whose favourite sport was rounders.

x) In Year 4, over half of the children chose rounders.

xi) In Year 6, 10 children preferred running.

xii) There were 261 children in the whole school.

  **QTS LITERACY TUTOR**
 **WWW.LITERACYSKILLSTEST.CO.UK**

★ ★ ★ ★ ★ Based on hundreds of reviews on ⭐ Trustpilot

FREE ONLINE LITERACY SKILLS TEST
EXPERT 1 TO 1 TUITION WITH OUR QTS SPECIALISTS

— WHAT QTS LITERACY TUTOR HAS TO OFFER —

Spelling Practice

Punctuation Questions

Grammar Section

Comprehension Resources

Practice Tests

Expert Tutors

Correct Format

New Question Formats

Visit **www.literacyskillstest.co.uk** to take a **Free Full Practice Test today.**

10
LITERACY SKILLS TESTS

97%
LEARNER PASS RATE

490
TEST QUESTIONS

10.9   I can make inferences using a cumulative frequency graph

Cumulative frequency graphs show a running total which is plotted on the Y axis. In the numeracy skills test the cumulative frequency often represents the number of students in a given context. You can determine averages using these curves and make a number of inferences.

Explanation Example

The graph below shows the ICT Test Marks of 30 pupils.

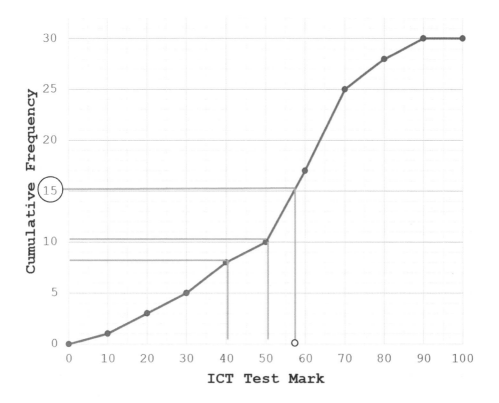

Question 1: How many people scored 50 marks or fewer?

Looking at the 50 mark on the x – axis we can go up the cumulative frequency line and look across at the y-axis and see that **10** people scored 50 or fewer on the test.

Question 2: How many people scored 40 marks or fewer?

Similarly, looking at the 40 mark, we see that 8 people scored 40 or fewer. We can use this information to work out that **2** people scored between 41 and 50.

Question 3: Calculate the range of marks

Looking between 90 and 100 we see the graph is flat indicating that no one scored between 91 and 100.

The range of scores is **90** (90 − 0).

Question 4: Calculate the median mark

To find the median we need to half the total number of people: 30 ÷ 2 = 15. The median is the 15th person's score. Therefore, going along from 15 to the curve then down to the x-axis we can estimate the median mark to be **57**.

Question 5: Find the upper and lower quartile

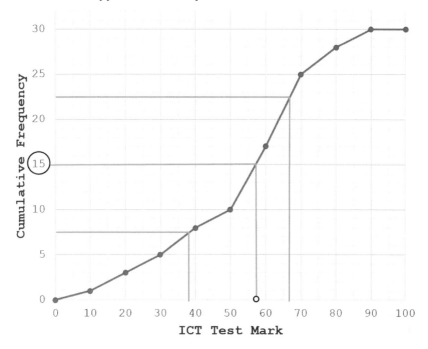

ICT Test Mark

To find the lower quartile we need to find ¼ of the total number of people. The lower quartile in this example is the 7.5th persons score, going along from there, to the line then down to the x-axis we can estimate the lower quartile mark as 38.

To find the upper quartile we need to find 3/4 of the total number of people. The upper quartile in this example is the 22.5th persons score; going along from there to the line then down to the x-axis we can estimate the upper quartile mark as 66.

Question 6: Find the inter-quartile range.

To find the inter-quartile range we subtract the lower quartile from the upper quartile.

66 – 38 = **28**

10.10 I can make inferences using a cumulative frequency graph – TEST questions

a) The graph below shows the times taken for 38 people to complete a race.

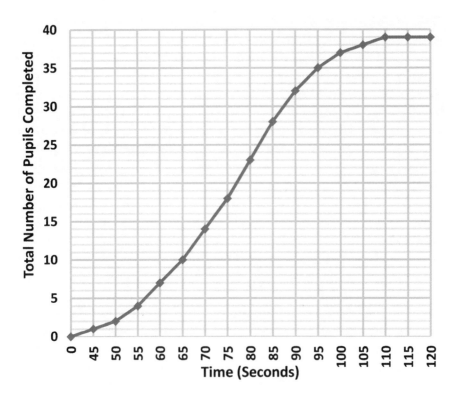

Select all **TRUE** statements from the list below:

i)	No pupils finished the race in under 45 seconds.
ii)	The slowest person finished in less than 110 seconds.
iii)	In total 40 people ran the race.
iv)	The median can be estimated at 60 seconds.
v)	The lower quartile is 50 seconds.
vi)	90 seconds for the upper quartile.
vii)	18 pupils finished in 75 seconds or less.
viii)	No pupils finished in the interval 55 to 60 seconds.
ix)	Three pupils finished between 90 and 95 seconds.

b) The graph above shows the amount of time that a group of students spend revising.

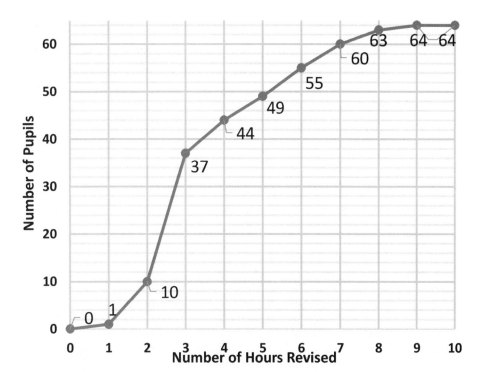

Select all **TRUE** statements from the list below:

i)	There were 64 pupils in the group.
ii)	No pupils revised more than 10 hours.
iii)	10 pupils revised for 2 hours or fewer.
iv)	18 pupils revised from 2 to 3 hours.
v)	No pupils revised for less than one hour.
vi)	No pupils revised for more than 9 hours.
vii)	The median can be estimated at 2 hours and 45 minutes.
viii)	The upper quartile suggests that 75% of people revised for under 4 hours.
ix)	Twice as many people revised between 5 and 6 hours than between 7 and 8 hours.

10.11   I can make inferences using a pie chart

Pie charts are a good way of presenting different proportions of data, as at a glance you can see the largest and smallest sections and compare these to another pie chart if required. It is important to note, two pie charts might represent different numbers of people/students etc but appears the same size and therefore may not be directly comparable at a glance.

Explanation Example

This pie chart shows the GCSE choices of 26 pupils

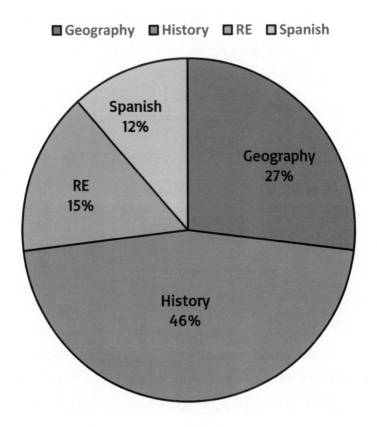

History is the most popular choice of subject with 46% of people choosing it; geography second; RE third and finally Spanish.

Example Question 1: Calculate how many students study each subject:

We can work out the amount of people studying each subject by calculating a percentage of an amount.

- History - **46% of 26 = 0.46 × 26 = 11.96 =** 12 people
- Geography - **27% of 26 = 0.27 × 26 = 7.02 =** 7 people
- RE - **15% of 26 = 0.15 × 26 = 3.9 =** 4 people
- Spanish - **12% of 26 = 0.12 × 26 = 3.12 =** 3 people

Example Test Question 1: Calculate the percentage point difference between geography and history.

This question refers to percentage points, rather than percentage change. This means we need to look at the percentages as numbers and find the difference between the numbers.

We can see that geography is 27% and history is 46%, so we must find the difference between these numbers.

$$46 - 27 = 19 \text{ percentage points}$$

Example Test Question 2: Find the fraction of students who studied RE, give your answer in its simplest for.

We know that 15% of students chose RE. 15% can also be written as $\frac{15}{100}$ (Remember percentages are out of 100)

Next, we need to simplify the fraction. We can do this by dividing the top and bottom by 5.

$$\frac{15}{100} = \frac{3}{20}$$

10.12 I can make inferences using a pie chart – TEST questions

a) The pie charts below display a school's GCSE subject choices.

2014 has 62 GCSE students.

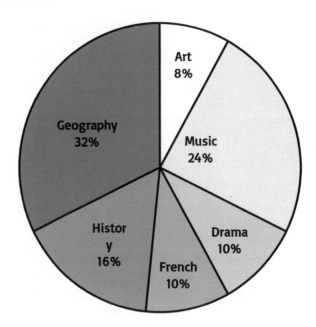

2015 has 81 GCSE students

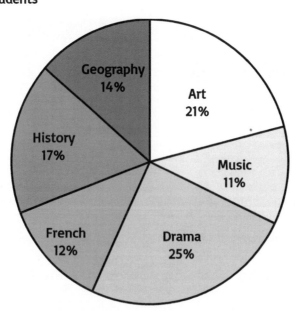

Select all **TRUE** statements from the list below:

i) Twelve fewer people chose art in 2014 than in 2015.

ii) Drama was the most popular subject across both years.

iii) 3/7 of people in both years two chose art.

iv) In 2014, 8/25 people chose geography.

v) Twice as many people in school A chose music than in school B.

vi) One tenth of people chose drama in school A.

vii) The number studying history increased by 40% from 2014 to 2015.

viii) The number studying art decreased by 40% from 2014 to 2015.

ix) One quarter of people chose drama in school B.

x) Across both years 20 people studied French.

xi) Three times as many people studied drama in 2015 compared to 2014.

xii) geography was the least popular subject in 2015.

b) The university choices of 193 A level students are displayed below.

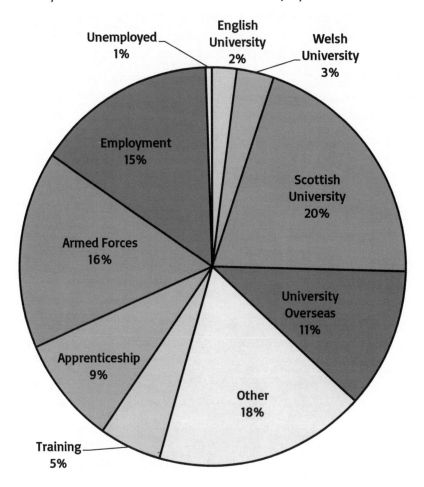

Select all **TRUE** statements from the list below:

i) More people attended universities outside of Scotland than in Scotland.

ii) Three people became unemployed.

iii) Seventeen people went onto an apprenticeship.

iv) One fifth of students went to a Scottish university.

v) Unemployment was the smallest destination.

vi) 9/50 of people went to Other destinations

vii) The most popular destination. was to attend a Scottish University.

viii)   The range of number of people to each destination was from 1 to 39.

ix)   0.15 of people went in employment.

x)   Eight times as many people joined the armed forces than went to an English University.

xi)   Thirty-seven people were in other.

xii)   1/5 of people went into Training.

10.13　I can make inferences using a two-way table

Introduction

Generally, one-way tables are just a way of showing the raw data. Two-way tables are a way of summarising data in number form.　Like we saw in some of the graphs, we can have say test scores and then break this down by subject or by gender and easily compare the data presented.

Explanation Example

The table below shows the percentage of students who passed English, maths and science exams over a three year period for two separate schools.

Acorn School

Year	English (%)	Mathematics (%)	Science (%)
2015	75	74	73
2016	71	73	76
2017	72	73	79

Beech College

Year	English (%)	Mathematics (%)	Science (%)
2015	63	72	78
2016	68	65	73
2017	72	67	69

What these tables show:

In 2016, 76% passed science at Acorn School

In 2015, 63% passed English at Beech College.

Example Test Question 1: Calculate the percentage point difference between the numbers of people who passed mathematics at Acorn School in 2015 to 2017.

This question refers to percentage points, rather than percentage change. This means we need to look at the percentages as numbers and find the difference between the numbers.

We can see that mathematics in 2015 is 74% and mathematics in 2017 73%, so we must find the difference between these numbers.

$$74 - 73 = 1 \text{ percentage point}$$

Example Test Question 2: In which year did Beech College have the greatest range of passes across all three subjects?

For this we need to work out the rank of pass percentages across all three years. This is the highest pass percentage – Lowest pass percentage.

2015: 78 - 63 = 15

2016: 73 - 65 = 8

2017: 72 - 67 = 5

From this we can see the year with the greatest range is **2015**

10.14 I can make inferences using a two-way table – TEST questions

a) The test results of 5 schools in the Yora Academy Trust are displayed in the table below.

	Average End of Year Test Percentage (%)				
English Faculty	Alfarm	Betrum	Calmwall	Dentons	Ebolt
Drama	71	93	64	42	51
English Language	73	87	53	63	61
English Literature	78	87	72	69	62
Mathematics Faculty					
ICT	84	66	79	72	60
Further Mathematics	80	53	50	58	42
Mathematics	82	72	64	63	62

Select all **FALSE** statements from the list below:

i)   The English Faculty at Betrum outperformed the mathematics faculty in every subject.

ii) Across all five schools, ICT had the highest mean mark.

iii) Pupils at Denton studying drama had a higher average mark than at Ebolt.

iv) The ICT average score for Betrum was 10% higher than Ebolt.

v)   Alfram had the highest range of scores across the 6 subjects.

vi) The lowest average score was for further mathematics at Ebolt.

vii) The mean English Language Score in the region was 73.6

viii) The mean English Language Score was higher than the mean English Literature score.

ix) The range of marks for the mathematics Faculty at Calmwall was 29.

x)   For the entire region, the median drama score was 64.

xi) At Alfram all pupils taking Further mathematics scores less than 80%.

xii) The highest Average Percentage was for Betrum's drama pupils.

b) The results of a repeated test for pupils in English intervention at Chalington Grange are displayed in the table below.

	Dec	Jan	Feb	Mar	Apr	May
Amy	64	66	71	80	88	93
Bella	64	65	66	69	72	74
Charlie	75	72	71	68	63	60
David	50	60	42	66	64	67
Eric	41	48	63	65	64	68
Felicity	47	51	53	55	54	59

Select all **FALSE** statements from the list below:

i)   David and Eric have the same mean score across the 6 months.

ii)   January had the lowest range of scores of any month.

iii)   Bella has the smallest range of scores.

iv)   Felicity's mean score was 82.

v)   Amy scored more than 80 in 1/3 of the months.

vi)   Charlie's score constantly increased.

vii)   March and April have the same range of scores.

viii)   Amy's mean score was 77.

ix)   February had a mean score of 52.

x)   The maximum score was 88.

xi)   In December, the median score was 57.

xii)   The minimum score was 41.

11. Other Data interpretation questions

The numeracy skills test contains a few very unique topics which you may never have encountered before. In this section you will see explanations of these topics and examples to help you understand how to answer these questions in your actual exam.

11.1 I can work with formulas and weighting Introduction

There are a number of formulae that appear in the numeracy skills test. These are given to you at the start of a question and you then have to use the data provided and substitute values into the formula in order to calculate the correct answer.

Explanation Example

The final mark for an English qualification is based on the formula shown below. Use this and the table to answer the following questions.

$$\text{Final mark} = \frac{(Oral) + (2 \times Reading) + (3 \times Writing)}{6}$$

Student	Oral	Reading	Writing
J	75	73	68
K	58	61	83

Example 1: Calculate the final mark for student J

By substituting the text for the relevant values, we can obtain values for the final mark.

$$\frac{(75) + (2 \times 73) + (3 \times 68)}{6} = \frac{425}{6} = 70.83$$

Student J final mark = **70.83**

Example 2: Calculate the final mark for student k

By substituting the text for the relevant values, we can obtain values for the final mark.

$$\frac{(58) + (2 \times 61) + (3 \times 83)}{6} = \frac{429}{6} = 71.5$$

Student **K** final Mark = **71.5**

Thus we can see that student K achieved the highest mark.

11.2   I can work with formulas and weighting – TEST questions

a)   The final marks for an English qualification are given using the following
     formula:

$$Final\ mark = (0.8 \times Test\ 1\ mark) + (0.2 \times Test\ 2\ mark)$$

The results of three students are shown below.

	Test 1	Test 2
Amber	64	52
Ben	63	64
Charlie	56	93

Work out who achieved the highest final mark using the formula.

b)   Mrs Haltby needs to convert 203 degrees Fahrenheit to Celsius. She is told
     that to obtain the temperature in Celsius she must:

Take 32 away from the Fahrenheit temperature.

Then, times the answer by 5.

Then, divide this answer by 9.

Work out the temperature in Celsius.

c)   Using the following area for a triangle work out how much bigger than
     15cm^2 a triangle of height 17cm, width 23cm is.

$$Area\ of\ triangle = \tfrac{1}{2} \times height \times width$$

d) The one hundred and one pupils in Year 3 at Corkridge Primary were asked how many siblings they each have. The data collected is displayed in the table below.

No. of siblings (S)	Frequency (F)	S × F
1	47	47
2	24	48
3	16	
4	14	
Sum	101	

The mean number of siblings can be calculated by dividing the sum of the S × F column by the number of pupils.

Complete the table and calculate the mean number of siblings, rounding your answer to two decimal places.

e) The formula for working out the final mark for the French GCSE is given by:

$$\frac{(2 \times \textit{Writing Test Mark}) + \textit{Oral Test Mark} + \textit{Listening Test Mark}}{4}$$

Using the scores of Sharon and Tanya given below work out the highest mark.

	Writing	Oral	Listening
Sharon	78	75	73
Tanya	74	79	83

f) The volume of a sphere can be calculated using the formula,

$$\frac{4}{3} \times 3.14 \times r \times r \times r$$

where r is the radius.

If the radius of a spherical desk globe is 4cm, work out its volume to the nearest 3 decimal places.

g) Wilkinson's Academy Year 9s are going on a trip to the Eureka! National Children's Museum in Halifax. It took 30 minutes to complete the journey.

Journey	Miles
Wilkinson's to M62	2
M62 to A629	6
A629 to A6193	12.8
A6193 to Eureka!	2.1

The average speed can be calculated by the dividing the distance in miles divided by the time taken. Work out the average speed, in miles per hour, from the school to Eureka!

h) A school is calculating the cost of borrowing £10,000 in order to fund a revamp of its sports facilities. The interest the charity charges is 2% per year. The school intends to pay back the loan in one year.

The total amount the school has to pay back can be calculated using the formula below.

$$Total\ cost = A\ (£) \times (1 + P)$$

A = Amount borrowed

P = Percentage interest as a decimal

How much will the school have to pay back at the end of the year?

11.3 I can work out the best price when considering discounts and offers

Introduction

These questions appear in tables and you have to use the data to perform multi-step calculations which often require a comparison of prices or discounts.

Explanation Example

Greenhill Academy needs to buy 115 tables for classrooms in the new Sixth Form building. The two approved suppliers both have offers available as shown in the table.

Shop	Cost (£)	Offer	Shipping
TablePro	79	5 for 4	£5 per table
Furnitr	89	10 for 9	Free

Example Test Question: Work out which supplier offers the best value for money (including shipping costs).

1. First work out how many we need to pay for:

   TablePro

   $$\frac{4}{5} \text{ of } 115 = 92$$

   So we pay for 92 with table pro

   Furnitr

   $$\frac{9}{10} \text{ of } 115 = 103.5$$

   We pay for 104 with Furnitr

2. Work out the cost for the tables.

TablePro	Furnitr
$79 \times 92 = £7,268$	$104 \times 89 = £9,256$

3. Add the shipping

TablePro	Furnitr
$5 \times 115 = £575$	**Free Delivery**
$£7,268 + £575 = £7,843$	
Total Cost = £7,843	**Total Cost** = £9,256

From this we can see that **TablePro** is the cheaper option to order the 115 tables from.

11.4 I can work out the best price when considering discounts and offers – TEST questions

a) Work out how much cheaper it is to buy 14 packets of felt-tips from SuperStationer in comparison to BargainPens.

	Cost per pack (£)	Offer	Delivery
SuperStationer	1.99	Buy one get one free	£4.95
BargainPens	1.89	Three for two	Free

b) A school prints out 230 paper registers each day for 195 days a year. Each register costs £0.02. An annual subscription to a digital register website costs £73.95 each year. Work out which option, paper or online register copies, is cheaper and by how much.

c) A head teacher has to decide whether to employ a supply teacher at a cost of £32 per hour for 900 hours a year plus £450 finder's fee, or a full-time member of staff for 950 hours at a cost of £30 per hour. Which option is the most cost effective?

d) Thornbramble Elementary needs to purchase 14,000 workbooks for the next academic year. Using the schools purchasing system the administrator has produced the following table.

Supplier	Cost per 1000 (£)	Offer	Delivery
A	890	10% off	Free
B	840	Five for four	£3.99 per 1000
C	815	No offer.	Free

Which is the most cost effective option?

e) Cutting the school field each year costs £72 for each day it is cut by an external company for the first ten times, then £65 for each day after. The school requires the grass cutting 26 times a year. Alternatively, the school can buy a lawnmower at a cost of £2,199 and claim back 20% for VAT. Which is the most expensive option for the school over the period of 1 year?

f) A school canteen purchases 4000kg of potatoes per year. They can choose between two suppliers which are displayed in the table below.

Shop	Weight of bag	Cost (£)	Offer
PotatoChief	25kg	7.99	None.
FresherPotaoes	5kg	£1.95	Buy two, get one free.

Which is the cheapest supplier?

g) A printer costs £1,485 to buy, with each toner cartridge costing £56.00, on a buy two get one free offer. Each toner prints 10,000 sheets. Alternatively, the school can hire a printer at a cost of £0.01 per sheet printed. In one school year, the school prints 250,000 sheets. Which option is the cheapest for one year, purchase or hire?

h) Fleetwood High bulk buys school jumpers each year.

Size Cost (£)				
Shop	Small	Medium	Large	Offer
UniFormPro	7.99	7.99	7.99	10% off small jumpers
ClothingLtd	7.99	8.99	9.99	15% of total price

For the next school year, the school needs to purchase:

200 small,

650 medium,

and 400 large

Which shop, UniFormPro or ClothingLtd would be the cheapest option?

12. Full Practice Test

Visit **QTS Maths Tutor** to take our full free practice test in exam conditions.

These tests have been designed to mimic the real numeracy skills test as much as possible.

Just visit https://www.qtsmathstutor.co.uk/ and click **Free Practice Test**.

Looking for Literacy Skills Practise?

Visit: http://literacyskillstest.co.uk/ for practice tests, tutors and much more.

Take our **Free Literacy Skills Test** Now!

  **QTS MATHS TUTOR**
WWW.QTSMATHSTUTOR.CO.UK

FREE ONLINE NUMERACY SKILLS TEST
EXPERT 1 TO 1 TUITION WITH OUR QTS SPECIALISTS

— **WHAT QTS MATHS TUTOR HAS TO OFFER** —

**21 Numeracy
Skills Tests**

**12 Topic
Revision Tests**

**Over 120
Video Solutions**

**Regularly Updated
Questions**

**Expert 1 to 1
Tuition Service**

**Written Solutions
to every question**

Visit www.qtsmathstutor.co.uk to take a **Free Full Practice Test today.**

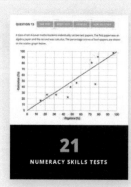

21
NUMERACY SKILLS TESTS

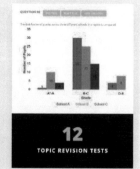

12
TOPIC REVISION TESTS

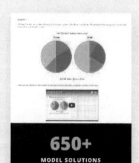

650+
MODEL SOLUTIONS

 **QTS LITERACY TUTOR**
WWW.LITERACYSKILLSTEST.CO.UK

★ ★ ★ ★ ★ Based on hundreds of reviews on  **Trustpilot**

FREE ONLINE LITERACY SKILLS TEST
EXPERT 1 TO 1 TUITION WITH OUR QTS SPECIALISTS

— WHAT QTS LITERACY TUTOR HAS TO OFFER —

Spelling Practice

Punctuation Questions

Grammar Section

Comprehension Resources

Practice Tests

Expert Tutors

Correct Format

New Question Formats

Visit www.literacyskillstest.co.uk to take a _Free Full Practice Test today._

10
LITERACY SKILLS TESTS

97%
LEARNER PASS RATE

490
TEST QUESTIONS

The QTS Literacy Test

The QTS literacy test is divided into four sections: spelling, punctuation, grammar and reading comprehension. Unless you have special arrangements, you have 45 minutes to complete the test. The total number of marks available in the test is between 45 and 49 and is broken down as follows:

Spelling – 10 marks

Punctuation – 15 marks

Grammar – 10 – 12 marks

Reading Comprehension - 10 – 12 marks

The pass mark of the test does vary slightly according to the difficulty of the test but is normally set around the 65% mark.

The spelling section is the only part of the test which you cannot revisit once you have submitted your answers. You can review your answers in the other three sections, meaning that if you are struggling with a given question, you can flag it, move on, and come back to it later, time permitting of course.

13. Spelling

- Questions: 10
- Marks: 10
- Percentage of paper: 20% - 22%
- Recommended time spent on this paper: 5 minutes
- What is considered a good mark for this section? 8 or above

The spelling section has to be completed first, and is the only part of the test that cannot be revisited once you have finished it. The reason for this is that the word you have been asked to spell could appear in a text later in the test, therefore giving the answer away.

In this section of the test, you have ten sentences, each with one word missing. You have to listen to the missing word by clicking on an audio icon, and then have to type this missing word in the box provided. You are able to listen to the word as many times as you like, and I would recommend listening to it numerous times just to check that you are certain of the word you are being asked to spell.

There is also a non-audio version of the test where you have to select the correct spelling of the word from a list (similar to the spelling questions in the mock tests in this book). If you are eligible for the non-audio version, then make sure that you have made special arrangements for this in advance.

I have heard people say that they are 'naturally bad spellers'. Unless you are dyslexic, then you are not naturally bad at spelling. It is more likely that your school or college neglected to point out your errors of usage, or failed to teach them. Do not allow yourself to have a fixed mind-set on this and believe that, with a bit of practice, you can make improvements on your spelling!

With a bit of work on the spellings of the more difficult words (since these are the words that you are more likely to be tested on), and applying some of the general rules that I have included below, you should be looking to tackle this part of the test with confidence, and achieving full marks is certainly a possibility. Remember too that the DfE (Department for Education) does not provide a list of words to test you on; however, the words that you are going to be tested on are likely to be words which you might use in your professional role, words which you would conceivably use if you were writing to a parent or colleague, or writing an end of year report for a student (so the word 'cemetery' is probably not a word to be too concerned about, whereas a word like 'differentiation' might be). On the QTS

Literacy Tutor website, there is a list of recommended words to study for the spelling section. Google 'QTS Literacy Tutor Spelling' and you will find the spellings on the website.

Here are some general spelling 'rules', but remember that there are frequent exceptions to these rules.

13.1   Spelling tip 1: 'i' before 'e', except after 'c'

If people only remember one spelling rule, then it is this one. If you don't know this rule, remember that if a word has the letters 'i' and 'e' together, then the letter 'i' comes before the letter 'e', except when following the letter 'c'.

believe ('i' before 'e')

piece ('i' before 'e')

conceit ('i' before 'e', except after 'c')

receipt ('i' before 'e', except after 'c')

However, this rule only applies when the sound is an 'ee' sound. When the 'i' and the 'e' come together and do not make an 'ee' sound, then the 'i' comes after the 'e'

beige ('i' after the 'e' because the sound is not 'ee')

neighbour ('i' after the 'e' because the sound is not 'ee')

There are exceptions to this rule, like the word 'caffeine'. While the substance itself may be very useful in the teaching profession, it is unlikely to be a word you need to write all that often as a teacher, so therefore highly unlikely to appear in the test.

13.2 Spelling tip 2: 'y' becomes an 'i'

When a word ends with the letter 'y' in the singular form, the 'y' changes to an '-ies' in the plural:

body – bodies

lady – ladies

supply – supplies

difficulty - difficulties

However, this rule does not apply to words that end in a vowel and a letter 'y':

one day – two days

one way – many ways

This 'y' becoming an 'i' rule also affects verb forms too:

I try – he tries

we fly – she flies

It also affects suffixes (endings):

apply – application

fancy - fanciful

13.3   Spelling tip 3: dropping the letter 'e'

If you are adding a suffix (e.g. '-ing', '-able', '-ible', '-ion', '-tion', '-ous') to a word which ends with the letter 'e' and the suffix begins with a vowel, then you drop the 'e'.

hope – hop**ing**

adore - ador**able**

procrastinate – procrastinat**ion**

relate – relat**ion**

However, the letter 'e' is not dropped when the word ends in '-ce' or '-ge'. If the letter 'e' were dropped, then the word would be pronounced with a hard 'c' or 'g', which would be wrong:

advantage – advanta**geous**

peace - pea**ceable**

13.4   Spelling tip 4: consonant doubling rule

This rule helps explain why some words have a double consonant when a suffix is added, and why others do not:

stop – sto**pp**ed (doubling)

work – wor**k**ed (no doubling)

In a word with one syllable, you need to double the final consonant if the word ends in one vowel and one consonant:

chat – cha**tt**ing

cram – cra**mm**ing

grip - gri**pp**ing

In a word with more than one syllable, double the final consonant if the word ends in a vowel and a consonant, and the final syllable is stressed:

beGIN – begi**nn**ing (consonant doubled because final syllable is stressed) preFER – preferring (consonant doubled because final syllable is stressed)

BENefit – benefited (consonant not doubled because final syllable is not stressed)

Note that the consonants 'w', 'x' and 'y' are never doubled.

However, for words that end in the letter 'l', you do double the 'l' even if the stress does not fall on the last syllable.

cancel – cancellation

model – modelling

enrol – enrolling (however the word 'enrolment' only has one 'l' because this rule of doubling the letter 'l' only applies when you are adding a suffix beginning with a vowel)

13.5　　Spelling tip 5: adding '-ful'

Do not confuse the spelling of the word 'full' (not empty) which has a double 'l' with the suffix '-ful' which always has a single 'l':

doubt**ful**
colour**ful**
peace**ful**

However, the suffix '-fully' has a double 'l':

hope**fully**
peace**fully**

13.6　　Spelling tip 6: adding prefixes

It is highly likely that you will be asked to spell at least one word which contains a prefix. A prefix is added to the beginning of a word to amend its meaning, often to make the word have the opposite meaning.

happy – **un**happy

There are lots of different prefixes, the most common being: 'un', 'il', 'im', 'ir', 'mis' and 'dis'.

Do be careful with the prefix 'mis', which has a single letter 's' and not a double (think of the word 'mistake' which has one 's' and not two).

The key thing to remember is that when you add a prefix to a word, you may end up with a double letter. There is no need to drop a consonant. Note how the following words have a doubling of the consonant when the final letter of the prefix and the first letter of the root word are the same:

necessary – unnecessary (un + necessary)

satisfied – dissatisfied (dis + satisfied)

legal – illegal (il + legal)

relevant – irrelevant (ir + relevant)

legible – illegible (il + legible)

Words like 'unnecessary' and 'dissatisfied' are often misspelled (as is the word 'misspelled' by the way!) and could feature in the spelling section of the test, so remember that it is a double and not a single consonant when you attach the prefix.

13.7　Spelling tip 7: sound it out!

Try breaking down words in your head to help you decode the spelling. A word like 'meticulous' can be problematic to spell, but if you say it to yourself, slowly, syllable by syllable, hopefully you will imagine the word as:

me / ti / cu / lous

However, this example does also have a complicated '-ous' ending which can be easy to get wrong.

complimentary – com / pli / men / ta / ry (remembering that it is an '-ary', not '-ery' ending)

implementation – im / ple / men / ta / tion (remembering that a '-tion' ending is used for the sound is 'shun')

detrimental – de / tri / men / tal (remembering that the ending is '-tal', not　'-tel' or '-tle') subsequently – sub / se / quent / ly (remembering that it is a '-que' not a '-cue')

particularly – par / ti / cu / lar / ly (remembering that it is '-lar-' and not '-ler-')

administrative – ad / min / i / stra / tive

capabilities – ca / pa / bil / i / ties (remembering that when a noun ending in 'y' in the singular changes to an '-ies' in the plural)

Breaking the words down to individual syllables can be a helpful technique but, as you can see from several of the examples above, it is still not a guarantee that the spelling is obvious!

13.8   Spelling tip 8: words with double consonants

Words which have a doubling of a consonant can be very challenging to spell, particularly if there are multiple consonant doublings, as there are no set rules. The words 'agree' and 'aggressive' have the same 'ag' sound for the first syllable, but there is one 'g' in 'agree', but two in 'aggressive'. The most common double letter combinations are 'll' (e.g. parallel), 'ss' (e.g. possession), 'ee' (e.g. attendee), 'oo' (e.g. cooperate), 'ff' (e.g. differentiation), 'pp' (e.g. opportunity), 'rr' (e.g. irregular), 'mm' (e.g. communication).

Many words have a double consonant due to the addition of prefixes and suffixes (as described in earlier tips).

Remember that all words ending in '-ally' have a double 'l'.

Here is a list of problematic words. They are problematic because they have double consonant combinations, or because people think they should when they don't!

challenge	collaboration	syllable
intelligence	miscellaneous	colloquial
embarrassing	happening	millennium
occurrence	questionnaire	successful
difference	profession	accomplishment
personnel	recommend	fulfil
unnecessary	occasionally	occurred

13.9   Spelling tip 9: words that end in '-ance' and '-ence'

Words with these endings are often misspelled because these words endings sound the same when spoken. One way of working out the correct ending is to think of the verb that forms the basis of the '-ance' or '-ence' word.

If the verb ends in '-y', '-ure', '-ate' or '-ear', then the '-ance' ending is used:

comply – compliance

endure – endurance

tolerate - tolerance

appear – appearance

If the ending follows a hard 'c' or 'g', then '-ance' is used:

significance

elegance

If the verb ends in '-ere', then the ending will be '-ence':

adhere – adherence

interfere – interference

If the final syllable of a verb that ends in '-er' is stressed, then the ending is   '-ence':

refer – reference

confer – conference

If the word ends with an '-ide', then use '-ence':

confide - confidence

reside - residence

If the word ends with a soft 'c' or 'g', then use '-ence':

intelligence

innocence

If these words were spelt with the '-ance' ending, then the letters 'c' or 'g' would be pronounced with a hard sound, which would be wrong.

13.10 Spelling tip 10: words that end in '-ant' and '-ent'

These endings behave in a similar way to the rules for '-ance' and 'ence'.

If the verb ends in '-y', '-ure', '-ate' or '-ear', then the '-ant' ending is used:

comply – compliant

tolerate – tolerant

If the ending follows a hard 'c' or 'g', then '-ant' is used:

significant

elegant

If the ending follows a soft 'c' or 'g', then '-ent' is used:

decent

intelligent

diligent

If the ending follows an '-er' then '-ent' is used:

inherent

coherent

If the word ends with an '-id', then use '-ent':

confide - confident

reside - resident

13.11   Spelling tip 11: words that end in '-able' and '-ible'

An easy way to find out whether a word should be spelled with the '-able' or '-ible' ending is to remove this ending. Once you have removed the '-able' or '-ible' ending, are you left with an English word? If you are, then it should be '-able'. If not, it should be '-ible'.

breakable – take off the '-able' or '-ible', and you are left with the word 'break'. Since 'break' is a word in its own right, we must use the '-able' suffix.

acceptable – take off the '-able' or '-ible', and you are left with the word 'accept'. Since 'accept' is a word in its own right, we must use use the '-able' suffix.

visible – take off the '-able' or '-ible', and you are left with the word 'vis'. Since 'vis' is not a word in its own right, we must use the '-ible' suffix.

If you remove the suffix and you are left with a non-word that ends with a hard 'c' or 'g', then the suffix is '-able':

amicable (despite the fact that 'amic' is not a word in its own right)

13.12   Spelling tip 12: words that end in '-ary', '-ery' and '-ory'

Most words that take the '-ery' suffix are related to words that end in '-er':

miser – misery

discover – discovery

archer – archery

If you take the suffix off and you are left with a recognisable English word, then usually '-ery' is the correct suffix:

rob – robbery

forge – forgery

scene – scenery

If there is a similar word that ends in '-ion', then you should use the suffix   '-ory':

introduction – introduc**tory**

explanation – explana**tory**

conservation – conserva**tory**

If you remove the suffix and the word is not recognisable, then use the suffix '-ary'

vocabul**ary** ('vocabul' is not a word)

necess**ary** ('necess' is not a word)

Note that there are exceptions to these rules!

For spelling tips 9 – 12, there are a lot of rules to memorise so, rather than trying to memorise them all, perhaps a better strategy would be to learn how to spell a selection of the examples I have provided which you can apply to the words which may appear in the test.

13.13   Spelling tip 13: mnemonics and tricks

For those particularly challenging words, it may be worth thinking of mnemonics or other tricks to ensure that you can remember the spellings.

'Rhythm' is a really treacherous word, and a music teacher from my previous school taught the students the following mnemonic:

Rhythm **H**elps **Y**our **T**wo **H**ips **M**ove

'Stationery', in the school equipment sense, was always a word I could never spell, as I mixed it up with the word 'stationary', meaning 'not moving'. To help me remember that it was '-ery' and not '-ary', I thought up a little trick: knowing that a pencil is a piece of school equipment, and that there is an 'e', but no 'a' in 'pencil', this helped me to remember that it was 'stationery' with an 'e' and not 'stationary' with an 'a'. It really doesn't matter how pathetic the trick you make up is, and if it's one that you think of yourself, then it should be easier to remember. With a bit of imagination you should be able to think of something to help you spell any of those words that you find particularly difficult.

13.14   Tips for spelling practice

1. Get someone to test you. Give someone (perhaps someone who is in the same situation as you so you feel less awkward / embarrassed) a list of words that you are trying to spell correctly. Get them to read a word to you and you spell it back.   Make sure that the person testing you really focuses on your weaknesses; if you have spelled a word incorrectly, expect to be tested on this word repeatedly until you have mastered it.

2. Use a voice recorder. Record a list of words on your mobile phone. Play the list back to yourself, pausing after every word. Write the word down, and then compare to your original word list.

3. Look, say, hide, write, check. Take a quick look at the word, say it to yourself a few times, then write it and compare with the correct spelling. This is less effective than previous options since, by having a quick glance at the correct spelling of the word, you have cheated a little bit. However, every time you write a word accurately, you are embedding its correct spelling in your brain.

4. Flashcards. Write a sentence on the front of the flashcard which contains the word you are learning to spell, but leave a gap for the word that you are practising. Write down the missing word on a separate piece of paper and check with the reverse of the flashcard to see if the spelling is accurate. For example:
    the boy's b........... is starting to improve (front of flashcard)
    behaviour (back of flashcard)

5. Use the practice tests on QTS Literacy Tutor along with the practice papers on the DfE website to give you plenty of practise in the real exam format.

14.   Punctuation

- Questions: 1
- Marks: 15
- Percentage of paper: 30% - 33%
- Recommended time spent on this paper: 10 minutes
- What is considered a good mark for this section? 12 or above

The punctuation section of the test has the largest allocation of marks, so it is crucial to ensure that your revision for the test focuses on this. With a bit of practice, this should be a quick and easy way to score as close to full marks as possible.

In the punctuation section of the test, you are required to insert 15 punctuation omissions from a text. This does not necessarily mean that you have to insert 15 punctuation *marks* (missing commas, speech marks, question marks, colons etc.); a punctuation omission can also include the capitalisation of a lower case word and the creation of a new paragraph.

Below is a list of the 12 punctuation options you will have, followed later by explanations and examples of how to use them correctly in practice questions.

- a full stop .
- a comma ,
- a question mark ?
- a colon :
- a semi-colon ;
- a speech mark (a double quotation mark) "
- an inverted comma (a single quotation mark) '
- an apostrophe (identical symbol to the inverted comma above) '
- a bracket (or)
- a hyphen -
- capitalisation of a word
- new paragraph //

Sometimes in the text, you may see two omissions together. If there is a missing full stop, then this is one omission and the capitalisation of the next word, which will be the first word of the next sentence, is a second omission. This is great as you are effectively getting two for the price of one. I only mention this because it is important that you recognise that this is two omissions rather than one (if you see this as only one omission, then not only will you waste time looking for a missing piece of punctuation which is not there, but you may also end up inserting an additional punctuation mark somewhere that is not required). Make sure you make 15 alterations to the text, no more, no less, if you wish to have the best chance of scoring full marks on this section of the test (and scoring full marks here is easily doable).

Please note that this is not a comprehensive guide on how to use punctuation, but more of a quick guide on punctuation to help you pass this section of the test with as little effort as possible.

14.1   Full stops

One of the most common punctuation mistakes concerns the use, or the lack of use of full stops. A full stop is required at the end of every sentence, and it is highly likely that there will be missing full stops in your QTS test. If you have spotted a missing full stop, this is great news, as you will probably also need to capitalise the word immediately following this full stop, meaning that you now have found two punctuation omissions. There may even be a missing full stop at the end of a paragraph, which should be relatively easy to spot. I would recommend that the first thing you do in the punctuation section is to quickly scan every paragraph to see if there are missing full stops at the end of them. If there are, then you have gained your first mark with minimal effort.

Helping people with full stops by telling them that a full stop is needed at the end of a sentence is probably not that helpful, since most people know this already. The problem is understanding what actually makes a sentence.

A sentence is one main idea, thought or feeling, a set of words which is complete in itself, and this set of words must also make sense. It will contain a subject (the person or thing that completes the action, e.g. the teacher, Gary, my mum, he, they etc.) and a verb (the action, or doing word). The sentence may also have an object (the thing the verb is being done to) and it may contain subordinate clauses (additional pieces of information which can be removed and the main clause still makes sense). Without wanting to go into unnecessary detail, here is an example of a sentence:

The dog, who is called Colin, ate the bone.

'The dog' is the subject of the sentence (it is the person / thing that did the eating), 'ate' is the verb (the action word) and 'the bone' is the object since it was the thing that was eaten. The phrase 'who is called Colin' is a subordinate or dependent clause, providing a bit of additional information, but this clause can be removed from the main clause, still leaving us with the complete sentence 'The dog ate the bone.'

Remembering that a sentence is a group of words which makes sense on its own, and which conveys one idea, thought or feeling, see if you can work out what is wrong with this example:

Grange Hill school has five non-negotiable classroom rules if these rules are broken, then students will receive a sanction

This example should be divided into two separate sentences as follows:

Grange Hill school has five non-negotiable classroom rules. If these rules are broken, then students will receive a sanction.

'Grange Hill....rules' makes sense on its own, and is one complete idea which tells the reader how many rules there are at the school. The second sentence 'If........sanction' also makes sense on its own and is a completely separate idea from the first sentence, since it tells us what happens if one of the five classroom rules is not followed. Since there are two separate ideas, a full stop needs to be inserted between them. A full stop is also required at the very end of the text, after the word 'sanction'.

If you were reading this sentence aloud to someone, you would most certainly pause between the words 'rules' and 'if', and this is another indication that a full stop is required.

However, some people might not use the correct punctuation mark, and might be tempted to use a comma instead of a full stop.

Let's take a look at another example:

The boy swore at the teacher he then kicked his chair over before storming out of the class.

Some people might attempt to correct this sentence by adding a comma between 'teacher' and 'he', but this is wrong:

The boy swore at the teacher, he then kicked his chair over before storming out of the class.

The sentence should be punctuated as follows:

The boy swore at the teacher. He then kicked his chair over before storming out of the class.

In this example, again, there are two complete and separate ideas. The first is the boy swearing at the teacher, and the second is the boy kicking a chair over. 'The boy swore at the teacher' makes sense on its own, so this is a sentence, therefore a full stop is needed. Inserting a full stop here means that the rest of the text from 'he' to 'class' must make sense on its own, which it does.

If you are not certain whether a comma or full stop is required, think how you would read the sentence aloud. Generally, you would take a quick pause for breath when there is a comma, but a full stop allows you to take a much longer break without disrupting the meaning:

The boy was walking down the street but went home as soon as the rain started.

The boy was walking down the street he went home when the rain started.

These sentences should read as follows:

The boy was walking down the street, but went home as soon as the rain started.

The boy was walking down the street. He went home when the rain started.

In the first example, the comma allows you to take a quick pause for breath (or a pause for dramatic effect), but the phrase 'but went home as soon as the rain started' is not a sentence as it does not make sense on its own, so a full stop would be incorrect here.

In the second example, the full stop allows you to take a big pause. You could even go and put the kettle on before coming back to read the next part 'He went home when the rain started'. This is because 'He went home when the rain started' makes sense on its own. It is a sentence, a new idea, so needs to be preceded by a full stop.

14.2   Full stop practice questions

1. If a student disrupts for a third time, move the student where possible be very clear that you have added a written comment in their planner.

2. Lend student equipment if they are not equipped for learning if they fail to return equipment, then issue the student with a detention slip.

3. Grange Hill School is a non-denomination secondary school for boys aged 11 to 18 years girls are welcome in the sixth form.

4. Stormzy will be coming into school this afternoon to talk about respect it will be a high-energy afternoon.

5. The school will be closing at 1.20 on Friday students on Free School Meals will be able to collect their meal at break.

6. Friday 23 November will be a designated INSET day students are not required to come into school on this day.

7. Please be aware that the autumn term ends on Thursday 20 December students are expected back on Monday the 7th of January.

8. We welcome girls from all cultures, backgrounds and beliefs the school has a long and distinguished history and has been educating local girls for over 250 years.

9. Our aim is to provide an outstanding education for boys who attend our school we have a strong commitment to the pursuit of learning.

10. It is our belief that boys flourish best in our single-sex environment we have an enviable academic record and are proud of our students' achievements.

11. Members of the Learning Support Team work with subject teachers to develop a range of teaching strategies and resources for use in the classroom they also support individual students in and out of the classroom.

12. The support team also provides assistance for those bilingual learners whose first language is not English support is provided both in the classroom and, when necessary, through withdrawal from normal timetabled lessons.

13. Grange Hill has an extremely successful Sixth Form our primary aim is to ensure that all students experience an academic education of the highest standard.

14. In the Sixth Form, our expectations are high, with senior students expected to operate as role models for students in the lower school this is reflected in the Sixth Form appearance policy.

15. The Sixth Form offers a wide range of Level 3 courses which are studied over two years we offer A levels and BTEC National Diplomas.

16. Students who have not reached 5 A*-C grades at Key Stage 4 can still enter the Sixth Form, taking a one-year Level 2 course upon successful completion, students are encouraged to progress on to the Level 3 courses for a further two years.

17. Our core business is to support the students who study here there are various pastoral structures in place to maximise the potential of our students.

18. As a Sixth Form student, your drive, imagination and energy dictate what happens on a day-to-day basis there is a vast array of opportunities in which to get involved students in the Sixth Form are given a lot more responsibility within the life of the school this involves the appointment of a Head Boy and one or two Deputies, who chair the School Council and can influence the day-to-day working of the school.

19. While there is, of course, a heavy emphasis on working hard, there is a fantastic social life within the Sixth Form the showpiece event is the Summer Ball, a formal event run by the students themselves students also organise inter-consortium activities and social events, including Christmas and Leavers Balls.

20. As part of the Central Consortium, girls are welcomed at Grange Hill although we believe that single-sex education is beneficial through to Key Stage 4, we value having mixed classes in the Sixth Form being a consortium helps us to do this.

14.3   Full stop practice answers

1. If a student disrupts for a third time, move the student where possible. Be very clear that you have added a written comment in their planner.

2. Lend student equipment if they are not equipped for learning. If they fail to return equipment, then issue the student with a detention slip.

3. Grange Hill School is a non-denomination secondary school for boys aged 11 to 18 years. Girls are welcome in the Sixth Form.

4. Stormzy will be coming into school this afternoon to talk about respect. It will be a high-energy afternoon.

5. The school will be closing at 1.20 on Friday. Students on Free School Meals will be able to collect their meal at break.

6. Friday 23 November will be a designated INSET day. Students are not required to come into school on this day.

7. Please be aware that the autumn term ends on Thursday 20 December. Students are expected back on Monday the 7th of January.

8. We welcome girls from all cultures, backgrounds and beliefs. The school has a long and distinguished history and has been educating local girls for over 250 years.

9. Our aim is to provide an outstanding education for boys who attend our school. We have a strong commitment to the pursuit of learning.

10. It is our belief that boys flourish best in our single-sex environment. We have an enviable academic record and are proud of our students' achievements.

11. Members of the Learning Support Team work with subject teachers to develop a range of teaching strategies and resources for use in the classroom. They also support individual students in and out of the classroom.

12. The support team also provides assistance for those bilingual learners whose first language is not English. Support is provided both in the classroom and, when necessary, through withdrawal from normal timetabled lessons.

13. Grange Hill has an extremely successful Sixth Form. Our primary aim is to ensure that all students experience an academic education of the highest standard.

14. In the Sixth Form, our expectations are high, with senior students expected to operate as role models for students in the lower school. This is reflected in the Sixth Form appearance policy.

15. The Sixth Form offers a wide range of Level 3 courses which are studied over two years. We offer A levels and BTEC National Diplomas.

16. Students who have not reached 5 A*- C grades at Key Stage 4 can still enter the Sixth Form, taking a one-year Level 2 course. Upon successful completion, students are encouraged to progress on to the Level 3 courses for a further two years.

17. Our core business is to support the students who study here. There are various pastoral structures in place to maximise the potential of our students.

18. As a Sixth Form student, your drive, imagination and energy dictate what happens on a day-to-day basis. There is a vast array of opportunities in which to get involved. Students in the Sixth Form are given a lot more responsibility within the life of the school. This involves the appointment of a Head Boy and one or two Deputies, who chair the School Council and can influence the day-to-day working of the school.

19. While there is, of course, a heavy emphasis on working hard, there is a fantastic social life within the Sixth Form. The showpiece event is the Summer Ball, a formal event run by the students themselves. Students also organise inter-consortium activities and social events, including Christmas and Leavers Balls.

20. As part of the Central Consortium, girls are welcomed at Grange Hill. Although we believe that single-sex education is beneficial through to Key Stage 4, we value having mixed classes in the Sixth Form. Being a consortium helps us to do this.

14.4   Full Stop Test tips

It is extremely likely that you will need to insert a full stop in the test, perhaps more than once.

Always check that there are full stops in obvious places, such as at the end of every paragraph, and at the end of the piece of text.

You will probably also need to insert a full stop where two sentences have been incorrectly joined together. Remember, a full stop needs to be placed where one idea ends and a second idea starts. Read the text and ask yourself where you would naturally stop: a stop is an indication that you have reached the end of a sentence.

14.5   Commas

The comma is a much misused piece of punctuation. Without wanting to get too caught up in unnecessary detail (although I will illustrate some of the key ways commas should be used below), roughly speaking (very roughly), a comma is used to denote a pause. Think about where you would pause if you were reading a sentence and place commas accordingly. A writer will place commas to tell you where to pause in a sentence so that you can take a breath (essential if you are reading aloud), or to pause so that the overall meaning makes sense.

Consider, where you would pause, if you were reading your sentence, and place commas, accordingly.

In the above example, the writer has put the brakes on too frequently and we do not need to be reminded to pause as frequently as this. Here, the commas have been thrown around like confetti! They have also been placed incorrectly, disrupting the flow and meaning of the sentence. Many people make this common mistake of using too many commas, in the hope that if they put enough commas in a sentence, then at least some will be in the right place.

This is how the above example should have been punctuated:

Consider where you would pause if you were reading your sentence, and place commas accordingly.

If I were reading this sentence aloud, I would naturally pause after the word 'sentence', possibly making use of this comma as an opportunity to take a breath if I were reading aloud, before continuing with the rest of the sentence.

Have you ever had to read a sentence a second time because, at the first attempt, it did not make sense or seemed strange? What goes through your mind when you read the following sentence?

Most of the time travellers worry about their luggage.

Do you not think that the insertion of a comma can completely change the meaning of this sentence?

Most of the time, travellers worry about their luggage.

The insertion of the comma means we should pause after the word 'time'. If there is no comma, we may read the whole sentence without pausing, and end up with quite a different sentence, possibly imagining Doctor Who fretting at an airport terminal because his Samsonite hasn't turned up.

Below are some general rules for comma usage. There is more to the comma than the below, but these are the basics and should be adequate for the purposes of the QTS test.

1.   Use a comma to separate items in a list.

     I am going to Tesco this evening to buy eggs, cheese, potatoes and cabbage.

     Each item in the list needs to be separated with a comma, with the exception of the item before the word 'and'. It is quite likely that you will need to do this in the punctuation section, although it is possible you may need to use a semicolon instead of a comma (see section on use of semicolons).

2.   Use a comma to separate two adjectives if you could insert the word 'and' between the two adjectives, or if you could reverse the adjectives without affecting the overall meaning. Here is an example:

     The teacher was a tall, old man.

     A comma is required between these two adjectives because the phrase can be written as follows:

The teacher was an old, tall man.
The teacher was a tall and old man.
Compare this with the following phrase:

I love hot beef soup.

In this phrase, there is no comma because it would not make sense to put the word 'and' in between the two adjectives. Nor would the phrase make sense if 'hot' and 'beef' were reversed:

I love hot and beef soup.
I love beef hot soup.

3. Use a comma after an introductory word or word group. This could be an introductory adverb such as 'furthermore' or a short phrase like 'at the end of the evening' or 'given the behaviour of the class'. This introductory element adds extra detail and, if you remove it, the rest of the sentence must make sense.

    Having analysed this year's results, I see a big dip in the performance of EAL students.

    If you remove the introductory phrase 'having analysed this year's results', the rest of the sentence is a complete sentence in its own right, so therefore the use of the comma is correct. Again, if you were reading this sentence aloud, you might pause after the word 'results', and a pause is usually a clue to comma usage, as stated above.

4. Use a comma when you join two sentences together with co-ordinating conjunctions (and, but, or, nor, for, so, yet).
    I like cheese.
    I don't like milk.

    Above are examples of two independent clauses. If we join them together with the word 'but', then a comma must be inserted before the conjunction.

    I like cheese, but I don't like milk.

Again, if you were reading this sentence aloud, you might pause after the word 'cheese', and a pause is usually a clue to comma usage, as stated above.

5. Use a comma to interrupt a sentence with additional information, especially if the interruption starts with the words 'who' or 'which'.

The boy, who attends my weekly intervention class, is now starting to make progress.

In this example, the original sentence is "The boy is now starting to make progress". Because we have interrupted this main sentence with extra information about him attending an intervention session, this extra phrase must have a comma both before and after it. Again, if you were reading this sentence aloud, you could pause after the word 'boy' and after the word 'class'.

6. Use a comma if you are joining a dependent clause to an independent clause. An independent clause is a group of words that can stand alone as a sentence and make sense, whereas a dependent clause does not make sense on its own. Here are two examples to illustrate the difference:

Please complete the attached reply slip. This is an independent clause as it can stand alone and make sense.

If you plan to attend Sports Day. This is a dependent clause as it does not make sense on its own. This clause will only make sense when added to another clause.

If the dependent clause comes first, use a comma.
If you plan to attend Sports Day, please complete the attached reply slip.
If the independent clause comes first, no comma is necessary.
Please complete the attached reply slip if you plan to attend Sports Day.

Again, think about where you would pause if you were reading. In the first example, you would probably pause between the words 'Day' and 'please', whereas in the second example, you would read the full sentence without pausing.

7. Use a comma after a salutation (a greeting) in a letter:

Dear Mr Smith,

8. Use a comma before opening speech marks and, in some situations, before closing speech marks (see section on inverted commas).

Make sure you understand the above rules. Remember that if you are uncertain about whether to use a comma or not, thinking about where you would naturally pause when reading the text aloud is a useful starting point.

14.6   Comma practice questions

1. The technology suite which is currently being redeveloped will be ready for September 2019.

2. Until the summer students are expected to wear a smart black blazer at all times.

3. Sadly the boys were outperformed by the girls for the sixth consecutive year.

4. Students will visit the Sagrada Familia Park Güell and of course Camp Nou the home of Barcelona Football Club.

5. In the school canteen you can have sandwiches snacks cooked meals and soft drinks.

6. In the second block of GCSE options students can choose a humanity a language technology or music.

7. Having observed Mr Smith today I have concluded that he needs to improve his use of questioning his behaviour management and his use of AfL.

8. Having paid an initial deposit parents should make arrangements to apply for an EHIC card.

9. As a result more target language needs to be used in modern language lessons.

10. There may however be occasions where a school will be forced to exclude students.

11. George's behaviour in maths is deteriorating making teaching and learning difficult in this lesson.

12. Students are expected to wear knee length grey skirts.

13. Olivia is not working to her potential in lessons nor is she completing homework on time.

14. Ben has received commendations from his teachers so he will be nominated for an end of year award.

15. There are however occasions where a TA may need to intervene.

16. On the other hand Leroy is making excellent progress in rugby even though his attendance in training is sporadic.

17. For example use your seating plan to learn the names of students as soon as possible.

18. Having already received a warning for talking Ben did not modify his behaviour.

19. Simon who is in the top set is an excellent choice for form captain.

20. These results which I am quite proud of are the rewards of all the extra work that I put in last year.

14.7   Comma practice answers

1. The technology suite, which is currently being redeveloped, will be ready for September 2019. *The main sentence has been interrupted with additional information using a 'which' clause, so this extra information needs a comma before and after it* (see rule 5).

2. Until the summer, students are expected to wear a smart, black blazer at all times. *A comma is required after the first introductory word group* (see rule 3). *A second comma is needed to separate the two adjectives that describe the blazer* (see rule 2).

3. Sadly, the boys were outperformed by the girls for the sixth consecutive year. *A comma is required after the first introductory word* (see rule 3).

4. Students will visit the Sagrada Familia, Park Güell and, of course, Camp Nou, the home of Barcelona Football club. *A comma is required to separate the first two items in the list, but note that there is no comma before the word 'and'* (see rule 1). *There is a comma before and after the words 'of course' since there is an interruption* (see rule 5) *and, finally, there is a comma after the word 'Nou' since additional information has been added here* (see rule 5).

5. In the school canteen, you can have sandwiches, snacks, cooked meals and soft drinks. *A comma is required after the first introductory word group* (see rule 3). *Commas are needed to separate items in a list, but note that there is no comma before the word 'and'* (see rule 1).

6. In the second block of GCSE options, students can choose a humanity, a language, technology or music. *A comma is required after the first introductory word group* (see rule 3). *Commas are needed to separate items in a list, but note that there is no comma before the word 'or'* (see rule 1).

7. Having observed Mr Smith today, I have concluded that he needs to improve his use of questioning, his behaviour management and his use of AfL. *A comma is required after the first introductory word group* (see rule 3). *Commas are needed to separate items in a list, but note that there is no comma before the word 'and'* (see rule 1).

8. Having paid an initial deposit, parents should make arrangements to apply for an EHIC card. *A comma is required after the first introductory word group* (see rule 3).

9. As a result, more target language needs to be used in modern language lessons. *A comma is required after the first introductory word group* (see rule 3).

10. There may, however, be occasions where a school will be forced to exclude students. *A comma is required before and after the word 'however' since this is an interruption to the main sentence* (see rule 5).

11. George's behaviour in maths is deteriorating, making teaching and learning difficult in this lesson. *A comma is required after the word 'deteriorating' since additional information is being added* (see rule 5).

12. Students are expected to wear knee length, grey skirts. *A comma is required here to separate two adjectives* (see rule 2).

13. Olivia is not working to her potential in lessons, nor is she completing homework on time. *A comma is required here before the conjunction 'nor'* (see rule 4).

14. Ben has received commendations from his teachers, so he will be nominated for an end of year award. *A comma is required here before the conjunction 'nor'* (see rule 4).

15. There are, however, occasions where a TA may need to intervene. *A comma is required before and after the word 'however' since this is an interruption to the main sentence* (see rule 5).

16. On the other hand, Leroy is making excellent progress in rugby, even though his attendance in training is sporadic. *A comma is required after the first introductory word group* (see rule 3). *A comma is also required after the word 'rugby' since additional information is being added* (see rule 5).

17. For example, use your seating plan to learn the names of students as soon as possible. *A comma is required after the first introductory word group* (see rule 3).

18. Having already received a warning for talking, Ben did not modify his behaviour. *A comma is required after the first introductory word group* (see rule 3). *You could perhaps argue that this is an example of a dependent clause followed by an independent clause* (see rule 6).

19. Simon, who is in the top set, is an excellent choice for form captain. *The main sentence has been interrupted with additional information and a 'who' clause, so this extra information needs a comma before and after it* (see rule 5).

20. These results, which I am quite proud of, are the rewards of all the extra work that I put in last year. *The main sentence has been interrupted with additional information using a 'which' clause, so this extra information needs a comma before and after it* (see rule 5).

14.8   Comma Test tips

It is highly likely that you will be required to insert commas in the text. I would estimate that you will need to add between two and four commas in total.

It is more likely that you will need to use commas to separate items in a list, or to separate two adjectives.

If the text is a letter, you might need to insert a comma at the end of the opening salutation.

In addition to this, it is likely that you will need to use commas after introductory information in sentences, or to separate additional information. Think about where you would pause for breath as a reader, as this is an indication that a comma may be required.

If you think you have punctuated the text to the best of your ability, but you know you are missing a couple to make your tally of 15, then it is quite likely that you have missed some commas.

14.9   Question marks

The use of the question mark is very straightforward, certainly as far as the QTS test is concerned. If the sentence asks a question, then it needs to end with a question mark. In written English, questions are constructed in two ways:

1.   The sentence starts with a question word like 'how', 'why', 'who', 'where', 'when', 'what':

How do you tackle the issue of transgenderism in the classroom?

2.   The sentence starts with the words 'do, 'does' or 'did':

Do you think your lessons lack pace?

3.   The order of the words changes and the verb comes before the subject:

Have you ever considered leaving the profession?

If there are questions in the text which you have to punctuate, it is quite common that the question is the main heading of the text, or possibly a sub-heading. It could also be the opening sentence of a paragraph, where a problem is suggested which is then followed up by some solutions:

Is teacher workload affecting your work-life balance? If this is the case, then here are some pieces of advice for you......

Question marks are used inside speech marks if the words that are being spoken form a question (see below section on how to use speech marks), although it is unlikely that this will be a consideration in the test, since the texts are factual pieces of writing, and not stories with characters. However, it is conceivable that there could be a quote from a person in the form of a rhetorical question.

"Do you genuinely believe that I would exclude poorly-behaved children just because we have an Ofsted inspection?" said Mr Griffiths in response to allegations that many pupils were asked not to attend St Mary's School on the day that Ofsted were planning to visit.

Do not be tempted to add question marks for indirect questions:

The teacher asked if Ofsted would be providing lesson feedback.

14.10   Question Mark Test tips

You may not need to use the question mark in the test, but if you do, it is unlikely that you will use it more than once. If you need to use question marks, they are more likely to be required in the title of the text or in the opening sentence of a paragraph.

14.11   Colons

Understanding how to use a colon correctly is not easy. However, let's make things as easy as possible with just a very brief explanation in terms of how you are expected to use a colon in the QTS test. In the literacy test, a colon is used before a list, and all the items that make up this list come after this colon (all the items in the list subsequently need to be separated by commas or semicolons – see sections on comma and semicolon use). Here is an example of a sentence which has a colon:

These are the field events that the pupils can take part in this year: hammer, shot put, discus, javelin, high jump, long jump, triple jump and pole vault.

In this example, there is a list of field events, so a colon is required before the start of this list (notice too how each item in the list has a comma after it, with the exception of the final item).

You might also see colons being used where there are paragraph titles / headings followed underneath by descriptions / clarifications. In these texts, it is highly likely that you will see other paragraph headings / sub-headings followed by colons, so all you have to do is spot that the pattern is consistent throughout the entire text:

Tennis:

Boys to wear white T-shirt, white shorts, school socks and trainers / plimsols

Girls to wear white T-shirt, white shorts or skirt, school socks and trainers / plimsols

Football

Boys to wear red school football shirt, white shorts, school socks and studded boots

Girls to wear yellow school football shirt, white shorts, school socks and astro trainers

In this example, there is a colon after 'tennis' followed by a description of tennis clothing, but there is no colon after the word 'football', so add a colon here to follow the previously established pattern. Always check for consistency in the text!

14.12   Colon practice questions

(Other punctuation will need to be added to these examples)

1. You may be required to bring many things sleeping bags pans utensils and warm clothing.

2. For next lesson, students will need to bring in the following items flour margarine sugar and vanilla essence.

3. We will be climbing the following mountains to raise funds for Children in Need Snowdon Ben Nevis and Scafell Pike.

4. These are the students who are on the shortlist for Student of the Year Martin Wheeler Ciara Smith Caroline Sargeant and David Thornley.

5. Abdullah Quershi gained a grade 9 in these subjects maths English IT French and triple science.

6. In the GCSE maths exam, you will need the following equipment pen pencil rubber calculator ruler protractor and a pair of compasses.

7. You need to know these verb tenses for the GCSE Spanish exam the present tense the past tense the future tense the conditional tense and the imperfect tense.

8. These British values need to be addressed in every assembly this year democracy rule of law individual liberty and mutual respect.

14.13　Colon practice answers

1. You may be required to bring many things: sleeping bags, pans, utensils and warm clothing.

2. For next lesson, students will need to bring in the following items: flour, margarine, sugar and vanilla essence.

3. We will be climbing the following mountains to raise funds for Children in Need: Snowdon, Ben Nevis and Scafell Pike.

4. These are the students who are on the shortlist for Student of the Year: Martin Wheeler, Ciara Smith, Caroline Sargeant and David Thonnley.

5. Abdullah Quershi gained a grade 9 in these subjects: maths, English, IT, French and triple science.

6. In the GCSE maths exam, you will need the following equipment: pen, pencil, rubber, calculator, ruler, protractor and a pair of compasses.

7. You need to know these verb tenses for the GCSE Spanish exam:　the present tense, the past tense, the future tense, the conditional tense and the imperfect tense.

8. These British values need to be addressed in every assembly this year: democracy, rule of law, individual liberty and mutual respect.

14.14　Colon Test tips

Don't overthink the colon!　In the QTS test, if you are required to use a colon, you are only likely to use it to introduce a list.　It could also be required after a word or phrase as a sub-heading or bullet point, but this should be obvious since you should see other sub-headings or bullet points punctuated in the same way.

14.15   Semicolons

Semicolons are also very difficult to use, but as far as the QTS literacy test is concerned, you will only encounter them, if you encounter them at all, in lists. I have mentioned in the comma section above that when you are writing lists, each item should be separated by a comma.

Here are my recommendations for House Captain: Bob, Gary, Fred and Steve.

The list is introduced by a colon and the items in the list are separated by commas. The items in the list are:

Bob

Gary

Fred

Steve

What if the list was as follows?

Bob, Turner House

Gary, Adam House

Fred, Brunel House

Steve, Shackleton House

The list would now read:

Here are my recommendations for House Captain: Bob, Turner House, Gary, Adam House, Fred, Brunel House and Steve, Shackleton House.

This list is very messy, and possibly confusing, as there are so many commas. You could also argue that 'Turner House' looks like one of the recommendations for House Captain.

When items in the list already contain commas, you should use semicolons rather than commas to separate the items.

Therefore the above example should read as follows:

Here are my recommendations for House Captain: Bob, Turner House; Gary, Adam House; Fred, Brunel House; and Steve, Shackleton House.

Generally speaking, if the list is slightly complicated you can justify the use of a semicolon over a comma. Note too that before the final 'and' in the list, there is another placement of a semicolon (in a list using commas, you would not use an additional comma before the final item), but it is unlikely that you will need to position a semicolon in this part of a list in the test. Here is another example of a complicated list:

A few items are required for this trip: a large rucksack for all of the equipment; a selection of ropes of various thicknesses; specialist rock-climbing shoes with rubber soles; and a head torch with extra batteries.

As I am sure you can appreciate, this list is much more complicated than the following list, which would only require commas:

A few items are required for this trip: a large rucksack, a selection of ropes, specialist rock-climbing shoes and a head torch.

I can imagine that you are asking yourself the question, "At what stage does a simple list become a complicated list?" Don't worry about it! In the QTS test, you will know to use semicolons rather than commas because it is likely that you will see other items in the list separated by semicolons. As I have said before, always check for consistency. If you see commas in a list, don't start adding semicolons and vice versa.

14.16   Semicolon practice questions

These examples are more challenging than the QTS test as there is a lot of punctuation missing. In the actual test, there will be far less missing punctuation than this, and the punctuation they have included will guide you as to how to complete the rest.

1. In today's meeting we have the following attendees Gary Smith University of Bristol Simon Jones University of Warwick Gemma Ledbury University of Hull and Steve Nichol University of Liverpool.

2. These are the boys that should go on report at the start of the summer term Reece James 23 negatives Ibrahim Abdullah 17 negatives Lindrit Emin 14 negatives and Nabil Syed 12 negatives.

3. This is the proposal for the upcoming trip to Paris The Eiffel Tower an opportunity to take photos of this famous landmark the Louvre a chance to see the famous Mona Lisa the Catacombs a chance to see an underground burial site and Notre Dame a spectacular Gothic church.

4. We will need the following equipment for the Duke of Edinburgh expedition tent which needs to be waterproof sleeping bag which should be suitable for temperatures down to 10 degrees first aid kit waterproofs which should have taped seams and walking boots which should be waterproof and comfortable.

5. This is a breakdown of what was collected for Children in Need by Year 7 7A £34 7B £76 7C £35 and 7D £64.

6. The following offences will result in a student being placed in isolation bringing the school into disrepute smoking including use of e-cigarettes criminal damage theft verbal abuse to staff and inappropriate use of mobile phones.

7. All our school rewards are issued as follows stamps recorded in planners by subject teachers reward postcards sent home on termly basis phone calls home made when pupils have achieved 50 stamps and certificates issued in end of term assemblies.

8. These are the classroom non-negotiables arrive on time be equipped for learning respect teachers by doing as you are asked, first time every time always do your best put your hand up and wait for permission to speak and always do your homework

9. This is step 4 of the behaviour system write third comment in planner fill in yellow detention slip enter a negative on school database issue work to student and send student to withdrawal room.

10. During form time we expect tutors to check planners discuss the thought of the day conduct uniform checks read relevant notices select a pupil of the week and have conversations with students who are routinely late.

14.17   Semicolon practice answers

1. In today's meeting we have the following attendees: Gary Smith, University of Bristol; Simon Jones, University of Warwick; Gemma Ledbury, University of Hull; and Steve Nichol, University of Liverpool.

2. These are the boys that should go on report at the start of the summer term: Reece James, 23 negatives; Ibrahim Abdullah, 17 negatives; Lindrit Emin, 14 negatives; and Nabil Syed, 12 negatives.

3. This is the proposal for the upcoming trip to Paris: The Eiffel Tower, an opportunity to take photos of this famous landmark; the Louvre, a chance to see the famous Mona Lisa; the Catacombs, a chance to see an underground burial site; and Notre Dame, a spectacular Gothic church.

4. We will need the following equipment for the Duke of Edinburgh expedition: tent, which needs to be waterproof; sleeping bag, which should be suitable for temperatures down to 10 degrees; first aid kit; waterproofs, which should have taped seams; and walking boots, which should be waterproof and comfortable.

5. This is a breakdown of what was collected for Children in Need by Year 7: 7A, £34; 7B, £76; 7C, £35; and 7D, £64.

6. The following offences will result in a student being placed in isolation: bringing the school into disrepute; smoking, including use of e-cigarettes; criminal damage; theft; verbal abuse to staff; and inappropriate use of mobile phones.

7. All our school rewards are issued as follows: stamps recorded in planners by subject teachers; reward postcards sent home on termly basis; phone calls home made when pupils have achieved 50 stamps; and certificates issued in end of term assemblies.

8. These are the classroom non-negotiables: arrive on time; be equipped for learning; respect teachers by doing as you are asked, first time every time; always do your best; put your hand up and wait for permission to speak; and always do your homework

9. This is step 4 of the behaviour system: write third comment in planner; fill in yellow detention slip; enter a negative on school database; issue work to student; and send student to withdrawal room.

10. During form time we expect tutors to: check planners; discuss the thought of the day; conduct uniform checks; read relevant notices; select a pupil of the week; and have conversations with students who are routinely late.

14.18   Semicolon Test tips

The semicolon can be difficult to use, but in the test it will be easy. If you need to use a semicolon, then it will be in a list. Use a semicolon when there is no punctuation mark between items in a list, but only if all other items in the list are separated by semicolons. Simply continue the pattern.

14.19   Speech marks (double quotation marks)

When you are writing, speech marks need to surround only the words that have been spoken by the person in the text. One set of speech marks needs to be inserted at the beginning of what was spoken, and a second set at the end of what was spoken. You will see numerous examples of speech marks in novels since there will no doubt be lots of direct speech between a story's characters. In the skills test, you will not be asked to punctuate an extract from the Da Vinci code, where there is dialogue between characters, but you might be asked to punctuate a short article about education in which there could be a quote from someone.

It also seems likely that, if you are required to use speech marks in the test, then one set of speech marks will already be given. Whenever you see speech marks in the text, immediately check to see if the speech marks are complete (in other words, is there a set of speech marks at the beginning of what was said and a second set at the end of what was said?). It is highly likely that if there is reported speech in the text, then one of the speech marks will be missing, and it is more likely that the second set of speech marks will be missing than the first set.

"We need to ensure that pupils from all social classes have the opportunity to succeed in school a government minister said.

In the example above, we can see that there is only one set of speech marks, so we know that we need to insert a second set somewhere, but where? We know the words that the government minister said. He said a total of 17 words, the first being the word 'we' and the final word being 'school', therefore the second set of speech marks needs to be after the word 'school'.

If the second set of speech marks is missing, then you may need to insert an additional punctuation mark before the closing speech marks, and this is the trickier part. You should insert a question mark if what was said was a question, an exclamation mark (although let's eliminate this as a possibility since you do not have the option of inserting exclamation marks in the literacy test), a comma or a full stop. In the above example, what was said was not a question, so we now need to choose between a comma and a full stop. Because the sentence continues with the words 'the government minister said' we use a comma, not a full stop. So the sentence should be punctuated as follows:

"We need to ensure that pupils from all social classes have the opportunity to succeed in school," a government minister said.

So there are two marks available here, one for the second set of speech marks and one for the comma before the speech marks.

Let's take a look if the sentence given had been presented like this:

A government minister said "We need to ensure that pupils from all social classes have the opportunity to succeed in school

Here, we again need to put a set of speech marks after the word 'school', as before. However, in this example, 'school' is the final word of the sentence (and is not followed by 'the government minister said') so here we would use a full stop. Remember, that the full stop, comma or question mark needs to come before the closing speech marks.

However, in this example we would also need to put a comma after the word 'said' so the example would be punctuated as follows:

A government minister said, "We need to ensure that pupils from all social classes have the opportunity to succeed in school."

To sum up this quite complicated point, this list should clarify:

1. Identify if it is the opening speech marks (the first set) which are missing or the closing speech marks (the second set).

2. If it is the closing speech marks that are missing (more likely), add the speech marks immediately after the final word that the person said. In addition, add a comma between the final word that was spoken and the closing speech marks if the final spoken word is not the final word of the overall sentence, or add a full stop between the final word that was spoken and the closing speech marks if the final word that the person said is also the final word of the overall sentence.

3. If it is the first set of speech marks that are missing, then simply insert an opening set of speech marks. If the speech marks are preceded by a phrase like 'Bob said', then you need a comma after the word 'said'. Remember too that the first word inside the speech marks needs to be capitalised.

Here are several examples for you to practise with. In these examples, there is no punctuation at all, which makes it even more challenging. As I mentioned above, it is more likely that, if you need to insert speech marks, you will only need to insert one set because the other set (probably the opening speech marks) will already be given.

14.20   Speech marks practice questions

1. One of my colleagues said to me if you had looked after your form group better, these problems wouldn't have arisen

2. The chances that they would do that on their own is negligible said Carrie Herbert, a former teacher.

3. We have saved children from ending up in gangs, and families from having breakdowns Herbert says.

4. Saunders says do we want them to leave with no self-esteem whatsoever

5. In response, Ferguson, the headteacher says all children at this school will be given the opportunity to succeed, so excluding them is not helpful to them in the long term

6. One small step for man, one giant leap for mankind were the famous words spoken by Neil Armstrong.

7. The headteacher started the assembly by saying the man who says he can, and the man who says he can't, are usually both correct

8. At the conference Chad Grylls said in its current state, what we call education is leading humanity towards extinction

9. Learning is not the product of teaching said Mr Holt it is the product of the activity of learners

10. Mr Simmonds addressed the audience at Open Evening and, controversially, proclaimed a child educated only at school is an uneducated child

14.21 Speech marks practice answers

1. One of my colleagues said to me, "If you had looked after your form group better, these problems wouldn't have arisen." *An opening set of speech marks is required before the word 'if' and a closing set after the word 'arisen'. The word 'if' requires capitalisation since it is the first word that was spoken. A comma is required after the phrase 'said to me'. A full stop is required before the closing speech marks because 'arisen' is the final word in the sentence.*

2. "The chances that they would do that on their own is negligible," said Carrie Herbert, a former teacher. *An opening set of speech marks is required before the word 'the' and a closing set after the word 'negligible'. A comma is required before the closing speech marks because 'negligible' is not the final word in the sentence.*

3. "We have saved children from ending up in gangs, and families from having breakdowns," says Herbert. *An opening set of speech marks is required before the word 'we' and a closing set after the word 'breakdowns'. A comma is required after the word 'breakdowns' because 'breakdowns' is not the final word in the sentence.*

4. Saunders says, "Do we want them to leave with no self-esteem whatsoever?" *An opening set of speech marks is required before the word 'do' and a closing set after the word 'whatsoever'. The word 'do' requires capitalisation since it is the first word that was spoken. A comma is required after 'says'. A question mark is required before the closing set of speech marks since this is clearly a question and not a statement.*

5. In response, Ferguson, the headteacher says, "All children at this school will be given the opportunity to succeed, so excluding them is not helpful to them in the long term." *An opening set of speech marks is required before the word 'all' and a closing set after the word 'term'. The word 'all' requires capitalisation since it is the first word that was spoken. A comma is required after 'says'. A full stop needs to be added before the closing speech marks because 'term' is the final word in the sentence.*

6. "One small step for man, one giant leap for mankind," were the famous words spoken by Neil Armstrong. *An opening set of speech marks is required before the word 'one' and a closing set after the word 'mankind'. A comma is required after the word 'mankind' since 'mankind' is not the final word in the sentence.*

7. The headteacher started the assembly by saying, "The man who says he can, and the man who says he can't, are usually both correct." *An opening set of speech marks is required before the word 'the' and a closing set after the word 'correct'. A comma needs to be added after the word 'saying'. The word 'the' needs to be capitalised since it is the first word that was spoken. A full stop is required after the word 'correct' since it is the final word of the sentence.*

8. At the conference, Chad Grylls said, "In its current state, what we call education is leading humanity towards extinction." *An opening set of speech marks is required before the word 'in' and a closing set after the word extinction'. A comma is required after the word 'said'. The word 'in' needs to be capitalised since it is the first word that was spoken. A full stop is required before the closing speech marks since 'extinction' is the final word of the sentence.*

9. "Learning is not the product of teaching," said Mr Holt, "It is the product of the activity of learners." *An opening set of speech marks is required before the word 'learning' and a closing set after the word 'teaching'. A comma is required before the closing speech marks since 'teaching' is not the final word of the sentence. A second opening set of speech marks is required before the word 'it' and a closing set after the word 'learners'. The word 'it' needs to be capitalised as it is the first word that is spoken in this group of spoken words. A comma is required after the phrase 'said Mr Holt'. A full stop is required before the second closing speech marks because 'learners' is the final word of the sentence.*

10. Mr Simmonds addressed the audience at Open Evening and, controversially, proclaimed, "A child educated only at school is an uneducated child." *An opening set of speech marks is required before the word 'a' and a closing set after the word 'child'. The word 'a' needs to be capitalised as it was the first word that was spoken. A comma needs to be inserted after the word 'proclaimed'. A full stop needs to be added after the word 'child' since this is the final word of the sentence.*

14.22   Speech marks Test tips

In the test, you may not need to use speech marks but, if you do, you will probably only need to add it once. You may also need to add other punctuation marks once you have added any missing speech marks.

You will know if speech marks are missing because one set, either the opening or closing speech marks, will already be given. All you need to do is work out where the spoken part of the sentence starts and ends.

If you are adding opening speech marks, then you need a comma before the speech marks (unless the sentence starts with speech marks), and the first word of the spoken part needs to have a capital letter.

If you are adding closing speech marks, remember that the speech marks need to go after the comma, full stop, question mark or exclamation mark (and it is possible that these commas, full stops and question marks may be absent too).

14.23   Inverted commas (single quotation marks)

Similar to speech marks, inverted commas come in pairs, so in the test, if you see one solitary inverted comma, you simply need to work out where the second inverted comma belongs. These inverted commas will be used to highlight the titles of books, films, plays etc. Here is a quick and easy example:

In year 10, all students will be required to study the novel 'An Inspector Calls. In year 11, they will move on to the Shakespeare play Macbeth'.

It is unlikely that you will have two examples of missing inverted commas in the text, but I have included two examples in one sentence simply to illustrate the point.

The sentence should read:

In year 10, all students will be required to study the novel 'An Inspector Calls'. In year 11, they will move on to the Shakespeare play 'Macbeth'.

Inverted commas simply require an eagle eye for detail. If you spot one inverted comma, check to see if there is a second one.

Note too, that full stops are placed outside the inverted commas since full stops are not part of the actual title. The same applies for any other punctuation marks (commas, exclamation marks, question marks, colons etc.). If they are not part of the title itself, then they do not appear inside the quotation marks.

Inverted commas can also be used to emphasise a word. This might be because the word is technical, unfamiliar or, more likely in the test, ironic:

John submitted his 'art' project late.

In this example, the word 'art' has been placed in inverted commas to create a sense of irony about John's ability as an artist. Clearly the project that John submitted is far from what the teacher deems to be 'art' in the real sense of the word. Can you imagine someone saying this sentence in an ironic way? Could you imagine the teacher even making an air quotation marks sign with his fingers when he says the word 'art'?

Some people are not sure when to use double or single quotation marks, but I wouldn't be too concerned about this in the test. Let's just assume that for the purposes of this test that the double quotation mark is used for direct speech, and single quotation marks for titles. Again, take your cues from what punctuation has already been given. If a title happens to have double rather than single quotation marks in front of it (I do not think this would be likely in the test as this would be incorrect), then it would be logical to use double quotations marks after it in order to keep the consistency.

Do not confuse inverted commas with apostrophes. Apostrophes are used for contractions (hadn't) or for possession (Steve's gloves). See my explanation of apostrophes for more guidance on this.

Here are a few quick examples, although these should be really easy!

14.24   Inverted comma practice questions

1. In order to boost some of our under-achieving pupils, the English department will be running an Easter invention session on King Lear.

2. In a recent article in The Independent, schools are being severely affected by budget cuts.

3. I think that all the students in the food technology group would benefit from watching The Great British Bake Off and Masterchef.

4. The latest Anthony Horowitz novel Scared to Death is now available in the library.

5. I recommend that all students read You are Awesome by Matthew Syed.

6. Tickets for Private Peaceful will be available for sale from Monday.

7. The year 11s are going to undertake a business project, very similar to one of the tasks seen on The Apprentice.

8. I am looking forward to tasting Paula's delicious brownies in food technology this afternoon!

9. Gary said that he was working but, to me, it looked like he was wasting time.

10. The handwriting in this exercise book is described by Luca as neat.

14.25   Inverted comma practice answers

1. In order to boost some of our under-achieving pupils, the English department will be running an Easter invention session on 'King Lear'.

2. In a recent article in 'The Independent', schools are being severely affected by budget cuts.

3. I think that all the students in the food technology group would benefit from watching 'The Great British Bake Off' and 'Masterchef'.

4. The latest Anthony Horowitz novel 'Scared to Death' is now available in the library.

5. I recommend that all students read 'You are Awesome' by Matthew Syed.

6. Tickets for 'Private Peaceful' will be available for sale from Monday.

7. The year 11s are going to undertake a business project, very similar to one of the tasks seen on 'The Apprentice'.

8. I am looking forward to tasting Paula's 'delicious' brownies in food technology this afternoon! *(Sarcastic use of 'delicious'. Clearly Paula has a reputation for not making very tasty brownies. You could also justify putting the inverted commas around the word 'brownies'. This would mean that they were definitely delicious, but perhaps not recognisable as brownies.)*

9. Gary said that he was 'working' but, to me, it looked like he was wasting time. *(Sarcastic use of the word 'working'. Gary's definition of what work is is clearly very different to what the speaker believes.)*

10. The handwriting in this exercise book is described by Luca as 'neat'. *(Sarcastic use of the word 'neat'. Luca's definition of what neat handwriting is is clearly very different to what the speaker believes.)*

Questions 8 – 10 are quite hard, and do make sense without the need for inverted commas. Remember that in the actual test, you have the added benefit of context, and one of the two inverted commas will invariably be given, meaning that a missing inverted comma around a word for emphasis will be much easier to spot.

14.26   Inverted comma Test tips

In the test, you may need to use an inverted comma, but it is unlikely to appear in every test. The lack of inverted comma should be easy to spot because they appear as a set of two, and you will probably just see one of them, so all you have to do is work out where the missing one belongs. Inverted commas belong before, and after, titles of plays, books and films.

You may need to put inverted commas around a phrase or word to draw attention to it, although this is less likely. Again, one of the inverted commas will be provided, so you simply need to work out where the other one belongs.

Do not confuse inverted commas and apostrophes. It is only inverted commas that come in pairs: apostrophes appear on their own.

14.27   Apostrophes

Apostrophes are extremely misused in the English language. Apostrophes should never be used when making a word plural! An apostrophe in a plural is probably the most common grammatical error made in the English language. It is not acceptable to write, "This shop sells sweet's and chocolate bar's....'. In this example both the nouns 'sweet' and 'bar' being used in their plural form, so 'sweets' and 'bars' is correct. Do not be tempted to add apostrophes to any plural words in your literacy test!

The apostrophe is used for contractions (a word which has been shortened and combines two words) and replaces a missing letter. Here are the most common contractions:

- From the verb 'to be': I'm / you're / he's / she's / it's / we're / they're / that's / who's
- From the verb 'to have': I've / you've / he's / she's / we've / they've

- For the word 'not': don't / doesn't / didn't / can't / won't / shouldn't / wouldn't / couldn't / mightn't / mustn't / wasn't / weren't / haven't / hasn't / hadn't / isn't / aren't

- For the word 'have': would've / could've / should've / might've / must've

- For the word 'will': I'll / you'll / he'll /she'll / it'll / we'll / they'll

- For the word 'would': I'd / you'd / he'd /she'd / we'd / they'd

- For the word 'had': I'd / you'd / he'd / she'd / we'd / they'd

The apostrophe is also used to indicate possession:

Simon's behaviour (the behaviour of Simon) *has been deteriorating since the start of the school year.*

The student's work (the work of the student) *was below the required standard.*

If the noun (item, object, thing) belongs to a singular person, then the apostrophe goes before the letter 's', but if the noun belongs to more than one person, then the apostrophe needs to go after the letter 's':

The boy's behaviour (the behaviour of the boy (singular)) *last week was disgraceful.*

The boys' behaviour (the behaviour of the boys (plural)) *last week was disgraceful.*

Be careful with irregular plurals such as 'men's coats' (the coats of men), 'women's rights' (the rights of women), 'children's behaviour' (the behaviour of children). (Never write ' mens' ' or ' childrens' '.)

The apostrophe is *not* used in these words: yours, his, hers, its (if 'it' means 'belonging to it' and not 'it is'), ours, theirs, but it is in one's (belonging to one).

14.28   Apostrophe practice questions

1. The school constantly monitor students attendance levels.

2. We ask that communication is maintained through the use of the students planner on a weekly basis and are always keen to address any issues which parents/carers may have. Should any students behaviour or progress become of concern, we will ensure that the issues are addressed.

3. The two principal components that drive our schools ethos are our commitment to academic success and to developing the individual.

4. The governments planned changes do not, for the time being, apply to Extended BTEC National Diploma courses.

5. Pastoral care is central to students progress and learning at Grange Hill.

6. In addition to places reserved for the schools own pupils, the governors propose to admit a minimum of 15 external students annually to its Sixth Form.

7. Appeals against an unsuccessful application should be made to the Schools Admissions Secretary who will arrange for an Independent Appeals Committee to hear the appeal.

8. Dont think you wont be caught; there are many ways to detect plagiarism. Remember, its your qualification so it needs to be your own work.

9. Its a shame that our school, despite its best efforts, cant find ways to improve certain students attitudes.

10. The childrens books had been marked according to school policy.

14.29   Apostrophe practice answers

1. The school constantly monitor students' *(the attendance of students)* attendance levels.

2. We ask that communication is maintained through the use of the student's planner *(the planner of the student)* on a weekly basis and are always keen to address any issues which parents/carers may have. Should any student's behaviour *(the behaviour of any student)* or progress become of concern, we will ensure that the issues are addressed.

3. The two principal components that drive our school's ethos *(the ethos of our school)* are our commitment to academic success and to developing the individual.

4. The government's planned changes *(the planned changes of the government)* do not, for the time being, apply to Extended BTEC National Diploma courses.

5. Pastoral care is central to students' progress *(the progress of students)* and learning at Grange Hill.

6. In addition to places reserved for the school's own pupils *(the pupils of the school)*, the governors propose to admit a minimum of 15 external students annually to its Sixth Form.

7. Appeals against an unsuccessful application should be made to the School's Admissions Secretary *(the Admissions Secretary of the school)* who will arrange for an Independent Appeals Committee to hear the appeal.

8. Don't think you won't be caught; there are many ways to detect plagiarism. Remember, it's *(contracted form of 'it is')* your qualification so it needs to be your own work.

9. It's *(contracted form of 'it is')* a shame that our school, despite its *(no apostrophe needed)* best efforts, can't find ways to improve certain students' attitudes (*the attitudes of certain students*).

10. The children's books *(the books of the children)* had been marked according to school policy.

14.30 Apostrophe Test tips

It is highly likely that you will need to add at least one apostrophe in the test. You are likely to have to insert an apostrophe where it has been omitted in a contraction (won't / can't etc.) or where there is an indication of possession. Be careful with the positioning of the possessive apostrophe where the noun is in the plural form (the boys' books = the books of the boys, the boy's books = the books of the boy).

Do not use apostrophes to make a noun plural!

14.31 Brackets (parentheses)

Opening bracket = (

Closing bracket =)

In the same way that inverted commas and speech marks should be easy to spot, brackets should also be easy. Brackets come in sets and, should you need to select brackets in the punctuation section, then it is likely that you will be given one of the brackets, meaning you simply need to work out where the other missing bracket belongs. If you are given an opening bracket, make sure you select a closing bracket and vice versa. It is highly unlikely that you would be asked to insert both an opening and a closing bracket, since the decision to use brackets or to not use brackets can be a matter of personal taste. However, if you see that brackets have been opened, they have to be closed, and if there is a closed bracket, there also needs to be an opening bracket.

Brackets are used to include extra information which isn't essential to the main point of the sentence. It could be an aside, or a quick phrase or short sentence to clarify something. You may have seen examples of this in the text (but if you haven't, then here is one for you right now!).

Here is an example of a sentence that could be part of the punctuation section in the test:

At Grange Hill School, our expectation is that all forms of low-level disruption (talking, fidgeting, pen-tapping, swinging on chairs, staring out of the window should be challenged by classroom teachers.

In this sentence, we first of all need to identify what is inside the brackets. In this example, inside the brackets are various descriptors of low-level disruption. All we need to do is work out when the low-level disruption examples stop before the sentence resumes. The final descriptor of low-level disruption is 'staring out of a window' so the closing bracket needs to come immediately after this.

At Grange Hill School, our expectation is that all forms of low-level disruption (talking, fidgeting, pen-tapping, swinging on chairs, staring out of the window) should be challenged by classroom teachers.

If you remove the bracketed section completely, the sentence needs to make sense, which it does:

At Grange Hill School, our expectation is that all forms of low-level disruption should be challenged by classroom teachers.

If you remove the bracketed section and it does not make sense, then you have not put the brackets in the correct place:

At Grange Hill School, our expectation is that all forms of low-level disruption (talking, fidgeting, pen-tapping, swinging on chairs, staring out of the window should be challenged) by classroom teachers.

If we remove the bracketed section, we are left with:

At Grange Hill School, our expectation is that all forms of low-level disruption by classroom teachers.

Since this sentence makes no sense when the bracketed section has been removed, this tells us that we have not positioned the brackets correctly.

14.32   Bracket practice questions

1. For the next charity drive, we would like all students to bring food items milk, jam, sugar, tea, coffee to help the homeless.

2. We would like all teachers of EBacc subjects English, maths, MFL, geography, history and science to attend the after school training session on Thursday.

3. Hassan new pupil from Somalia will need support in lessons since English is not his first language.

4. At Grange Hill School, pupils who represent the school for sport football, rugby, hockey, and athletics may receive a participation award at the end of term.

5. Education providers primary school, secondary schools, academies, pupil referral units will all be affected by the latest budget cuts.

6. Michael Gove the former Minister for Education made many controversial decisions which have negatively affected schools in our area.

7. The borough of Lewisham always seems to outperform other local boroughs Lambeth, Croydon, Southwark, and Bromley in terms of academic attainment.

8. Gary Smith winner of the Headmaster's Cup has turned down the offer of going to Cambridge and is going to read English at Durham.

9. We would like all members of staff to log all negative behaviours lack of planner, punctuality, uniform violations, low-level disruption, defiant conduct, aggressive behaviour, rudeness to staff on the new behaviour database.

10. Mrs Acaster local resident is always coming to the school to complain about the behaviour of our pupils at the end of the school day.

14.33   Bracket practice answers

1. For the next charity drive, we would like all students to bring food items (milk, jam, sugar, tea, coffee) to help the homeless. *In this example, examples of food items are put inside brackets to clarify the types of food items that the students are expected to bring in. Remove the bracketed part and the sentence still makes sense.*

2. We would like all teachers of EBacc subjects (English, maths, MFL, geography, history and science) to attend the after school training session on Thursday. *In this example, the bracketed section lists which subjects are included for the EBacc, in case there are teachers who are not aware what the EBacc includes. Remove the bracketed part and the sentence still makes sense.*

3. Hassan (new pupil from Somalia) will need support in lessons since English is not his first language. *In this example, clarification of who Hassan is is included in the bracketed section, in case there are teachers who need reminding who this student is. Remove the bracketed part and the sentence still makes sense.*

4. At Grange Hill School, pupils who represent the school for sport (football, rugby, hockey, and athletics) may receive a participation award at the end of term. *In this example, examples of the different school sports that the school participates in are listed for the benefit of the reader who may not be fully aware of the school's sport offering. Remove the bracketed part and the sentence still makes sense.*

5. Education providers (primary school, secondary schools, academies, pupil referral units) will all be affected by the latest budget cuts. *In this example, examples of the different types of educational providers are listed for the benefit of the reader who may not know which providers are going to be affected by the budget cuts. Remove the bracketed part and the sentence still makes sense.*

6. Michael Gove (the former Minister for Education) made many controversial decisions which have negatively affected schools in our area. *In this example, additional information clarifying who Michael Gove is is inserted in the brackets in case the reader has not heard of Michael Gove before. Remove the bracketed part and the sentence still makes sense.*

7. The borough of Lewisham always seems to outperform other local boroughs (Lambeth, Croydon, Southwark, and Bromley) in terms of academic attainment. *In this example, other London boroughs local to Lewisham are listed to highlight which ones Lewisham has outperformed. Remove the bracketed part and the sentence still makes sense.*

8. Gary Smith (winner of the Headmaster's Cup) has turned down the offer of going to Cambridge and is going to read English at Durham. *In this example, additional information about Gary Smith has been added. Here the bracketed section just adds weight to the fact that Gary Smith is clearly a very hard-working, intelligent student and reminds the reader who Gary Smith is, in case the reader was not sure who he was. Remove the bracketed part and the sentence still makes sense.*

9. We would like all members of staff to log all negative behaviours (lack of planner, punctuality, uniform violations, low-level disruption, defiant conduct, aggressive behaviour, rudeness to staff) on the new behaviour database. *In this example, examples of negative behaviours are put inside brackets to clarify the types of offence that are considered to be negative. Remove the bracketed part and the sentence still makes sense.*

10. Three boys in year 8 have been excluded, of which two (Reece Martins and Simon McPherson) are being questioned by police. *In this example, the names of the two boys who are going to be questioned by the police have been included in the bracketed section in case the reader wants to know their identity. Remove the bracketed part and the sentence still makes sense. You could justify the use of a comma here, but in the QTS test, you are likely to know to use brackets rather than commas because one of the sets of brackets will be provided for you.*

14.34   Bracket Test tips

In the test, you might need to add an opening or closing bracket. This will be obvious because brackets come in sets of two and you should spot quite easily that one of them is missing. All you need to do is work out what should be inside the brackets and position the missing bracket accordingly. Remember that if you were to completely remove the entire bracketed section from the sentence, the sentence needs to make sense.

14.35   Capitals

There must always be a reason for a capital letter. If you can't think of a reason, then keep the word in lower case.

A capital letter is always required to start a sentence and for proper nouns. Proper nouns include names of people, names of places (countries, cities, districts, planets), nationalities, languages, names of schools, names of companies, days of the week, months of the year, holidays (Easter, Christmas), titles of books, films, plays, songs.

Titles can be difficult to capitalise but, generally speaking, you should capitalise the first and last words of a title as well as any important words in between ('The Boy in the Striped Pyjamas'). Worrying about which words in a title are important for capitalisation purposes is likely to be beyond the scope of the QTS test.

You do not require capital letter for school subjects (science, maths, history), unless it is a language (French, Spanish, English) or it is an acronym (PSHE, DT).

You do not require capital letters for words like 'school', 'headteacher', 'borough', but these words would be capitalised in a title:

East Finchley Primary School
The Headteacher Mr Ferguson
The London Borough of Lewisham

In the QTS test, it is more likely that you will be capitalising a letter because you have already had to insert a missing full stop, but it is possible that there might be a missing capital letter at the start of a sentence / paragraph, or a missing capital letter in a title (although unlikely that you will need to capitalise more than one word in a title).

14.36   Capitals practice questions

1. pupil attainment is better in some parts of the Uk than others.

2. in the london borough of lewisham, there are several schools in special measures.

3. I have asked the class to watch 'wonder of the universe' this evening since the scientist brian cox will appear on it.

4. we are hoping that the school will appear in 'the yorkshire post' newspaper this evening.

5. my spanish class never do the homework i ask of them, but i know that some of them are watching 'narcos', which is better than nothing I suppose.

6. there are a few pupils in year 10 who are doing their work experience at boots.

7. some of our Eal students are performing below expectations.

8. since this is a roman catholic school, it is important that christmas is celebrated in the appropriate way.

9. the pupils always considered mr smith, the biology teacher, to be the most understanding.

10. i am happy that we don't need to teach latin in the school. trying to force the boys to engage with english and french is hard enough.

14.37   Capital practice answers

1. Pupil attainment is better in some parts of the UK than others.

2. In the London Borough of Lewisham, there are several schools in special measures.

3. I have asked the class to watch 'Wonder of the Universe' this evening since the scientist Brian Cox will appear on it.

4. We are hoping that the school will appear in 'The Yorkshire Post' newspaper this evening.

5. My Spanish class never do the homework I ask of them, but I know that some of them are watching 'Narcos', which is better than nothing I suppose.

6. There are a few pupils in year 10 who are doing their work experience at Boots.

7. Some of our EAL students are performing below expectations.

8. Since this is a Roman Catholic school, it is important that Christmas is celebrated in the appropriate way.

9. The pupils always considered Mr Smith, the biology teacher, to be the most understanding.

10. I am happy that we don't need to teach Latin in the school. Trying to force the boys to engage with English and French is hard enough.

14.38   Capital Test tips

It is likely that there will be a capitalisation error or two in the test. Scan through the text at the start to check that all paragraphs and sentences start with capital letters and check that there aren't obvious missing capital letters for people's names, book titles etc. Remember too that if you are inserting a full stop, you also need to amend the first word of the new sentence from lower case to a capital letter (and, as mentioned before, remember that this counts for two punctuation errors, not one).

14.39   Hyphens

The main purpose of a hyphen is to join two words together to form a compound word. The hyphen shows that the words joined together have a combined meaning and, on occasion, this can affect the overall meaning of a sentence.

Take a look at how the hyphen can change the meaning of the following two sentences:

I recently bought a little used bike.
I recently bought a little-used bike.

In the first example, the bike could be second-hand and small in size, whereas in the second example, because the words 'little' and 'used' have been linked together, we know that the sentence refers to a bike that has not been used very much (and this makes much more sense).

Although hyphen use can be quite complicated, missing hyphens should be relatively easy to spot in the QTS test because in the test, the word that requires the hyphen will be written as one word rather than two. For example, it might not be very obvious to you that the words 'little used' require a hyphen, but when it is written as 'littleused', which may look rather odd to you, hopefully you will quickly spot the problem.

Hyphens are most commonly used in compound adjectives (describing words), so be on the lookout in the QTS test for two adjectives which have been combined to form one word.
In the below examples, you should spot the missing hyphens quite easily because there are words which clearly need to be separated. Some of the words require more than one hyphen as well, although it is unlikely that in the test you will be required to add more than one hyphen in any compound word.

14.40   Hyphen practice questions

1. George is the fairhaired boy who sits at the back of the class.

2. The school banned all drinks from the canteen that were not sugarfree.

3. We have a custombuilt ICT suite on the new school site.

4. I always find George to be a very badtempered child.

5. If you opt for an apprenticeship, you are going to receive an abundance of onthejob training.

6. This new NQT is far too selfassured for my liking!

7. The content of this lesson is far too demanding for twelveyearold boys

8. Please read the uptodate guidance on how to move files from your laptop to the OneDrive.

9. The new building will be equipped with stateoftheart facilities.

10. This is not a oneoff incident: Jayden has displayed similar behaviour throughout the entire year.

14.41 Hyphen practice answers

1. George is the fair-haired boy who sits at the back of the class.

2. The school banned all drinks from the canteen that were not sugar-free.

3. We have a custom-built ICT suite on the new school site.

4. I always find George to be a very bad-tempered child.

5. If you opt for an apprenticeship, you are going to receive an abundance of on-the-job training.

6. This new NQT is far too self-assured for my liking!

7. The content of this lesson is far too demanding for twelve-year-old boys.

8. Please read the up-to-date guidance on how to move files from your laptop to the OneDrive.

9. The new building will be equipped with state-of-the-art facilities.

10. This is not a one-off incident: Jayden has displayed similar behaviour throughout the entire year.

14.42 Hyphen Test tips

There is a possibility that you will need to insert a hyphen in the punctuation text, but it is not a common feature of every test, and it is unlikely that you would need to add more than one. If you are struggling to find all 15 punctuation omissions, it could be that you have not spotted a missing hyphen somewhere. Go through the text again, looking for any large words that look unusual because they are a compound of two or more smaller words.

14.43   New paragraphs

Paragraphs break up a longer text into smaller and more manageable pieces. A paragraph is a distinct section of the text with a single theme or idea.

Let's take a look at a sample text:

Pastoral Support Managers are at the centre of all pastoral care within the school and should be the first point of contact for students and parents. They will deal with initial concerns or queries and investigate any incidents before referring matters to the appropriate House or Pastoral Leader. They will also liaise with individual subject staff and Curriculum Leaders to resolve any issues or concerns. In a minority of cases, they will also refer matters to the Deputy Head or other members of Senior Staff. House Leaders are responsible for establishing and promoting the positive day to day behaviour of students and for ensuring that each individual student makes a positive contribution to all aspects of school life; House Leaders promote engagement, participation, contribution and achievement and are responsible for maintaining the school's accepted standards at all times. Pastoral Leaders are responsible for supporting the progress and learning of all students and work specifically with the students who present any long-term educational or disciplinary concerns. In addition, the Pastoral Leaders monitor a wide range of indicators relating to students in their year group(s) including; attendance, punctuality, positive conduct, negative conduct, detentions, rewards and sanctions. Pastoral Leaders lead the tutor teams and uphold all school expectations.

The above piece of text is noticeably long, so long in fact that it is not appealing to a potential reader (did you even try reading it?), so this is a clear sign that there is poor paragraphing.

If we investigate this text, it begins by talking about the role and responsibilities of Pastoral Support Managers and then, on the 7th line, it starts talking about the roles and responsibilities of House Leaders. Since this is a change of theme, this should be a new paragraph. The same applies in the 11th line where the theme switches again from House Leaders to Pastoral Leaders, so this would also require a new paragraph:

Pastoral Support Managers are at the centre of all pastoral care within the school and should be the first point of contact for students and parents. They will deal with initial concerns or queries and investigate any incidents before referring matters to the appropriate House or Pastoral Leader. They will also liaise with individual subject staff and Curriculum Leaders to resolve any issues or concerns. In a minority of cases, they will also refer matters to the Deputy Head or other members of Senior Staff.

House Leaders are responsible for establishing and promoting the positive day to day behaviour of students and for ensuring that each individual student makes a positive contribution to all aspects of school life; House Leaders promote engagement, participation, contribution and achievement and are responsible for maintaining the school's accepted standards at all times.

Pastoral Leaders are responsible for supporting the progress and learning of all students and work specifically with the students who present any long-term educational or disciplinary concerns. In addition, the Pastoral Leaders monitor a wide range of indicators relating to students in their year group(s) including; attendance, punctuality, positive conduct, negative conduct, detentions, rewards and sanctions. Pastoral Leaders lead the tutor teams and uphold all school expectations.

By paragraphing in this way, the text is much more visually appealing to the reader, and reading the entire text now doesn't seem such an arduous task.

14.44   New Paragraphs Test tips

In the QTS text, take a look at the length of the whole text. If there is a lot of text together, this is probably a sign that more paragraphing is required. Not every test will require you to create new paragraphs but, if it does, it is highly unlikely that you will need to use the // symbol more than once.

14.45   Strategy

It is quite possible that, having read and understood the above (and answered all the practice questions!), you now feel confident to tackle the punctuation text without any further guidance. However, if you would like a scaffolded general strategy to ensure you get as close to full marks in this section as possible, then I would propose the following 3 stage strategy:

Stage 1

In stage 1, what I would propose is to scan through the text looking for the most obvious punctuation omissions. Look for full stops, brackets, speech marks, inverted commas and capitals. Perhaps a daft phrase such as "Fluffy Bears Steal Ice Creams" might be a useful (albeit daft!) sentence to help you remember what to look out for in stage 1.

Fluffy: F = full stops. Focus on the easy ones! Is there a full stop at the end of the text / at the end of each paragraph / at the end of each section?

Bears: B = brackets. Brackets come in pairs. Are there any missing opening brackets or closing brackets?

Steal: S = speech marks. Speech marks come in pairs. Are there any missing opening speech marks or closing speech marks?

Ice: I = inverted commas. Inverted commas come in pairs. Is there an opening or closing inverted comma missing?

Creams: C = capitals. Is the first word of each paragraph and each sentence capitalised? Are there any proper nouns missing capital letters (names of people, places, books, films etc.).

At the end of stage 1, you have hopefully picked up a few marks without having had to really exert yourself. Add up the punctuation changes you have made and work out how many more you have left to find. In stage 1, you have not really had to engage with the text and understand what it is about, you were simply looking for glaring punctuation errors.

Stage 2

Now that you know how many punctuation omissions you have left to find, you are going to have to read the text in a bit more detail and engage with what it is trying to convey. Stage 2 is all about lists, commas, full stops and question marks.

It is quite possible that, while you are reading the text, there are certain phrases that don't make sense. You might have to reread some lines to try and make sense of what the author is trying to say. If you are struggling to understand certain parts of the text, then this is a clue that there is a punctuation problem. It could be that you are misreading the text because a full stop has been left out, meaning you are reading two sentences as if they were one, or maybe parts of the text don't make sense unless you pause at a certain point. So, in this stage, look for missing full stops and obvious commas. Remember, you use a comma for a quick pause for breath, and a full stop for a complete break. Do not go comma crazy! Simply add the ones you are certain of at this stage and pick up any missing ones in the final stage.

In stage 2, look for lists as well. If you find a list, is it introduced by a colon? Is each item separated by a comma or semicolon? You shouldn't need to worry about whether to use a semicolon or comma as it should be obvious from the list: other items in the list will be separated by semicolons or commas, so simply continue the pattern.

Are there questions in the text which do not have a question mark at the end?

Again, tally up the new total of punctuation alterations and work out how many you still need to find.

Stage 3

Now that you have completed the very easy stage 1 and the slightly more complicated stage 2, hopefully you don't have too many more punctuation omissions left to find. At this stage, you might be starting to struggle to find the remainder, since the remaining omissions might be harder to spot.

Apostrophes – check for missing apostrophes. Are there contracted words with apostrophes missing (cant) or apostrophes missing where possession is indicated? Remember, do not be tempted to start adding apostrophes to plurals simply to boost your tally to the required 15!

Paragraphs – does the text look excessively long? Does any individual paragraph look excessively long? This could be an indication that a new paragraph needs to be created somewhere. Remember that a new paragraph is required when there is a change of theme.

Hyphens – if you are struggling to find the remaining punctuation omissions, then consider looking for individual words that should be hyphenated. Is there a word that looks a little odd? Is this word a combination of two words? If so, and you are running out of other feasible options, add a hyphen.

More commas – assuming you have not gone comma crazy in stage 2, then it is highly likely that the remaining punctuation marks are commas. Commas can be a matter of personal taste and style (which is why I recommended only putting in the obvious ones in stage 2), so go through the text looking for the most obvious places to position them. Remember that, in general, a comma can be justified if you were to pause when reading the text aloud. Look for pauses after introductory phrases, before and after words like 'however', 'in general', and before and after dependent clauses that add additional information, especially phrases starting with 'who' and 'which'.

14.46   Punctuation General tips

It may seem obvious, but do make sure that the punctuation you have spotted has actually been applied to the text. Don't assume that the apostrophe has appeared after you have clicked the apostrophe button, check that it is there, and check that it is in the position you intended as well!

When adding commas, make sure you put the comma in the correct place. Don't highlight a word and then just click the comma button, because this will automatically add a comma at the start of the word, whereas you will probably want to position the comma at the end of the word.

Make sure you make 15 alterations in total!

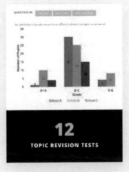

QTS LITERACY TUTOR
WWW.LITERACYSKILLSTEST.CO.UK

FREE ONLINE LITERACY SKILLS TEST
EXPERT 1 TO 1 TUITION WITH OUR QTS SPECIALISTS

--- **WHAT QTS LITERACY TUTOR HAS TO OFFER** ---

 Spelling Practice

 Punctuation Questions

 Grammar Section

 Comprehension Resources

 Practice Tests

 Expert Tutors

 Correct Format

 New Question Formats

Visit www.literacyskillstest.co.uk to take a Free Full Practice Test today.

10
LITERACY SKILLS TESTS

97%
LEARNER PASS RATE

490
TEST QUESTIONS

15. Grammar

- Questions: 3-4
- Marks: 10 - 12
- Percentage of paper: 20% - 26%
- Recommended time spent on this paper: 10 minutes
- What is considered a good mark for this section? 8 or above

The grammar section is a gap-fill exercise where you are presented with 3 texts (usually letters). In each text, there are between 3 - 4 questions, and for each question, you need to fill a gap in the text from one of the 3 - 4 options available. If English is your first language then, a lot of the time, some of the answers are reasonably obvious. If the correct answer is not obvious, then you may at least notice that there are some answers which are very obviously wrong, leaving you with fewer remaining options to guess from if required.

Below is a breakdown of the most common grammatical points that the test focuses on.

15.1 Grammatical point 1: inconsistency between subject and verb

Subjects and verbs have to agree with each other in terms of number. What this means is that a singular subject must have a singular verb and a plural subject must have a plural verb:

The cat is playing with the string. ('The cat' is singular so we need the singular form 'is' from the verb 'to be'.)

The cats are playing with the string. ('The cats' are plural so we need the plural form 'are' from the verb 'to be'.)

A lot of people mix up the verb forms 'was' and 'were', specifically using 'was' with a plural, which is incorrect:

There was a boy in the changing room. ('was' is singular because 'a boy' is singular)

There were two boys in the changing room. ('were' is plural because 'boys' is plural)

'There was two boys in the changing room' is completely incorrect and unacceptable.

Be careful when there are collective nouns (a class, team, group etc.). When a collective noun is used in the singular, then the verb is singular, even when the group contains more than one person:

35 hyperactive children are difficult to manage. (Plural verb because there is a plural subject)

15 girls were left in the hall. (Plural verb because there is a plural subject)

A class of 35 hyperactive children is difficult to manage. (Singular verb because 'a class' is singular.)

A group of 15 girls was left in the hall. (Singular verb because 'a group' is singular.)

When there is more than one subject, you need to use a plural verb, even if the item that precedes the verb is singular:

A positive mental attitude and a dictionary are all you need in my French lessons!

However, if the items are linked by the word 'or', then you would use the singular form of the verb:

A positive mental attitude or a dictionary is all you need in my French lessons!

When a sentence starts with each or every, the verb is singular:

Every child matters.

Each person in this class is responsible for their learning.

When there is an additional phrase or clause after the subject, the verb agreement can be hard to spot.

The teachers who attended the meeting were bored. (The verb must agree with 'teachers' which is plural. The verb does not agree with the singular word 'meeting'. Remember that it is the teachers that were bored, and not the meeting.)

The politics of the school were horrific. (The verb must agree with 'politics' which is plural. The verb does not agree with the singular word 'school'. Remember that it is the politics of the school that were horrific, not the school itself.)

Here is another example where there are potentially misleading options to choose from:

The headteacher, who is likely to be made redundant following allegations of unnecessarily excluding troublesome students, claims there has been no wrongdoing.

The headteacher, who is likely to be made redundant following allegations of unnecessarily excluding troublesome students, claim there has been no wrongdoing.

In a sentence like this, do not let a 'who' clause distract you from what the subject is. The subject is 'the headteacher' (singular) so the verb 'claims' must also be singular. Sometimes it is worth ignoring additional clauses, especially 'who' or 'which' statements, so that you aren't distracted from the main clause. In this example, it is not the students that are claiming, which is why the first and not the second example is correct.

Here is one final example:

I am particularly pleased by Gareth's attitude in science and maths which is very important as it shows he has taken on board what was discussed in our recent meeting.

I am particularly pleased by Gareth's attitude in science and maths which are very important as it shows he has taken on board what was discussed in our recent meeting.

If you don't give these questions the attention they deserve, you may think the first option is incorrect because the phrase '.....science and maths which is important' is not grammatically correct. You must comb through the text and work out what the subject of the verb is. What is important? Is it science and maths (plural) or is it Gareth's attitude (singular)? The final part of the sentence, 'as it shows....', tells us that it is Gareth's attitude that is very important in this sentence which is why the second example is correct.

It is very likely that there will be examples of subject and verb disagreement in your QTS test. Eliminate any examples where you see this!

15.2   Grammatical point 2: inconsistency with verb tenses

It is essential in the QTS test to ensure that you can recognise lack of consistency with verb tenses. It is acceptable to have different verb tenses in one sentence when the verbs refer to different periods of time. For example:

John was on target for a grade 7 last year, but he is currently working at a grade 4.

In this sentence, we have used the past tense 'was' to refer to what happened last year followed by the present tense 'is' to refer to what is currently happening.

If a sentence refers only to past events, then the past tense should be used throughout. It would be incorrect to say:

Last week, Gareth sat the maths test and achieves 56%.

This entire sentence refers to events in the past, so the past tense needs to be continued throughout in order to maintain verb tense consistency.

As far as the past tense is concerned, note that in English, there are two past tenses. One refers to a specific time in the past (the simple past tense: normally accompanied by a past tense time phrase such as 'yesterday', 'last week' etc.) and the other refers to an undefined time in the past (the past perfect: this tense will use the word 'have' or 'has').

Last year, I went to China.

Last year, I have gone to China.

In these examples, the second sentence is incorrect. When you refer to a specific time in the past ('last year' in this example), you use the simple past tense which is the past tense without the 'have' or 'has'.

If a sentence refers only to future events, then the future tense should generally be used throughout. It would be incorrect to say:

Next week, Simon will sit his maths GCSE and starts his part-time job the following Saturday.

This entire sentence refers to events in the future, so the future tense needs to be continued throughout in order to maintain verb tense consistency.

Verbs of hoping or looking forward can pose a problem as well. This is because you hope that something will happen in the future, or you look forward to something happening in the future. However, the actual act of hoping, or looking forward to something, normally occurs in the present, so a present tense is generally required.

I hope that I will succeed in my exams. (The succeeding is going to take place at some stage in the future, hence the future tense, but the hoping is happening in the present, hence the present tense. 'I will hope' would be incorrect in this example.)

I am looking forward to receiving my GCSE results and will be happy if I achieve a grade 5 in maths. (The being happy is going to take place at some stage in the future, hence the future tense, but the looking forward is happening in the present, hence the present tense. 'I will look forward' would be incorrect in this example. Note too that after 'if', English uses the present tense even though there is reference to a future action (this is different in other languages like French where it would be correct to use the future tense).)

There is a very high chance that you will see possible answers which contain verb tense inconsistencies, or answers which are inconsistent in tense to the question. These verb tense inconsistencies usually make the meaning unclear and confused, so are generally easy to spot. Make sure you read the options carefully and keep an eye out for any tense inconsistency.

15.3   Grammatical point 3: inconsistency in lists

When you see lists in the test, make sure that there is consistency in how each item is introduced.

This meeting is:

a) *an opportunity to raise important concerns about your upcoming appraisal and discussing how to set yourself measurable targets*

The above is a classic example of the type of incorrect option you could face. In this list, there are two key ideas being presented. The first is 'raising concerns' and the second is 'discussing targets'. However, both these items are presented differently in the list. What you have to do is analyse the sentence, and work out where in the sentence these two ideas attach to. In this example, the phrase 'this meeting is an opportunity to' is the phrase that both items are attached to. The first example 'raise important concerns' fits perfectly after 'an opportunity to', but the phrase 'discussing' simply does not fit after 'an opportunity to'. Therefore this answer can be eliminated and you should search for an answer where both list items do make sense after the phrase 'an opportunity to'. In this example, the correct answer would be:

This meeting is:

a) *an opportunity to* **raise** *important concerns about your upcoming appraisal and* **discuss** *how to set yourself measurable targets*

'Raise' and 'discuss' match in a grammatical sense, in a way that 'raise' and 'discussing' do not.

Here is another example:

Prior to the deadline of January 15, all year 10 boys are expected to:

a) *write an up-to-date CV; complete the work experience questionnaire; you should send in a scanned copy of your passport; read the Grange Hill Work Experience Handbook.*

Like the previous example, the items in this list are inconsistent. 'Write', 'complete' and 'read' are all grammatically similar verb forms which fit after the opening statement and after the word 'to'. However, 'you should send' does not match this consistency and when it is attached to this opening statement will read:

Prior to the deadline of January 15, all year 10 boys are expected to you should send in a scanned copy of your passport.

This clearly makes no sense whatsoever so can be eliminated. The correct option would read:

Prior to the deadline of January 15, all year 10 boys are expected to:

a) **write** *an up-to-date CV;* **complete** *the work experience questionnaire;* **send** *in a scanned copy of your passport;* **read** *the Grange Hill Work Experience Handbook.*

In this example, the four verb forms are consistent which means that the sentence now makes sense.

15.4 Grammatical point 4: misuse of should have / could have / would have / may have / might have

This is an extremely common error among English native speakers! So many people write 'should of' rather than 'should **have**', 'could **of**' instead of 'could **have**' and 'would **of**' instead of 'would **have**'. The reason for this common error is because we often use the contracted form 'should've' when we speak, and the shortening of the 'have' to ' 've ' sounds very much like the word 'of'. (Please note that, although the pronunciation of the ' 've ' in 'would've' might sound similar to 'of', it is not the exact pronunciation of the word 'of', whatever part of the English speaking world you come from! It should be said as more of an 'uv' sound than an 'ov' sound!)

In the test, discard every option where there is a 'should of', 'may of', 'could of' etc. These are all grammatically incorrect!

In some texts, you may see two separate and grammatically correct options, where the only difference is a difference in meaning because one sentence contains 'should have' and the other contains 'could have'.

'Could have' means that something was possible at some point in the past, but it did not happen:

Steve could have stopped the boy from falling.

In this sentence, it was possible for Steve to stop the boy from falling, but he didn't (for whatever reason).

'Should have' means that something did not happen, but we wish it had happened.

Mary should have called the police.

Mary did not call the police, and this was clearly a mistake or oversight on her part.

15.5   Grammatical point 5: and I / and me / and myself

There is a lot of confusion about whether you should use 'me' or 'I' in a sentence, but this confusion can easily be eliminated.

John and I went to the cinema.

John and me went to the cinema.

Which of the above is correct? The simplest way to check is to imagine how you would write this sentence if John hadn't gone to the cinema and the speaker had gone on their own. The sentences would read:

I went to the cinema.

Me went to the cinema.

Because it is grammatically correct to say 'I went to the cinema' and not 'me went to the cinema', that is why you would write 'John and I' and not 'John and me'.

This problem is less obvious when the person speaking is the object of the sentence:

Sue came to the cinema with John and I.

Sue came to the cinema with John and me.

Again, like the previous example, what would you write if Sue had gone to the cinema with the speaker and there was no John? The sentences would then read:

Sue came to the cinema with I.

Sue came to the cinema with me.

Because it is grammatically correct to say 'with me' and not 'with I', that is why you would have to write 'John and me' and not 'John and I' in this example.

As far as 'myself' is concerned, you cannot use it as a subject or object. These following sentences are not correct:

Steve and myself were interrogated by the headteacher.

Simon played football with Gary and myself.

These sentences should read:

Steve and I were interrogated by the headteacher.

Simon played football with Gary and me.

In the test, if you see an option with a 'myself' in it, it is highly likely that it can be discarded immediately.

15.6 Grammatical point 6: misuse of relative pronouns (who, whom and which)

'Who' and 'whom' are used to refer to people, not things, and the misuse of 'who' and 'whom' is very common. A lot of people use 'who' instead of 'whom', but this mistake is rarely noticed; it is almost as if this is an acceptable mistake to make. 'The boy who I saw....' is not grammatically correct English. It should be 'The boy whom I saw....'. (You might even think that the sentence sounds better with 'who' rather than 'whom', even though it is technically incorrect!)

Some people misuse the word 'whom' by using it when they should simply say 'who', and this is a mistake which is far more obvious. Certain people, if they are in a formal situation, or if they are wishing to give the impression of being more intelligent or educated, use 'whom' when they would usually say 'who'. Unfortunately, while the person may be trying to show off how educated they are by using 'whom' and not 'who', they might in fact be doing the opposite since they are making a glaring grammatical error.

Here is an example of 'whom' being incorrectly used:

We have decided to exclude your son, whom is not responding to our interventions, for three weeks.

The sentence should read:

We have decided to exclude your son, who is not responding to our interventions, for three weeks.

Let's make this explanation as simple as possible. If you are facing the choice between 'who' and 'whom', simply look at the next word in the sentence. If the word after 'who' or 'whom' is a verb, then use 'who'. If the word after 'who' or 'whom' is a new subject (another person), then use 'who'.

This is the boy whom we saw. ('Whom' because it is not followed immediately by a verb, but by a new subject 'we'.)

This is the boy who is top of the class. ('Who' because it is followed immediately by a verb.)

'Which' is used for objects and things, never for people:

The book, which is on the table, is the one the boy would like to read.

'What' should never be used in this context. Sentences of the type 'The boy what came to school', 'The book what is on the table' are ugly and wrong!

15.7   Grammatical point 7: these kinds / types / sorts of

You may be faced in the test with a set of options like this:

     a.   *these kinds of opportunity*
     b.   *this kinds of opportunity*
     c.   *these kind of opportunities*
     d.   *these kinds of opportunities*

If the noun being used is singular, then it should be preceded by 'this kind (singular) / sort (singular) / type (singular) of':

*This **kind** of **scheme***

*This **type** of **assessment***

*This **sort** of **feedback***

If the noun being used is plural, then it should be preceded by 'these kinds (plural) / sorts (plural) / types (plural) of':

*These **kinds** of **schemes***

*These **types** of **assessments***

*These **sorts** of **tests***

The same applies if the word being used is 'that' or those': 'that type of' followed by a singular noun and 'those types of' followed by a plural noun.

I would argue that it is possible to say 'these types of scheme' as well as 'these types of schemes' and that there is a subtle difference in meaning between the two, but as far as the test is concerned, rule out 'these types of' followed by a singular noun in favour of 'these types of' followed by a plural noun. Do be aware that there are many resources online and in other literacy books that have incorrectly explained this rule, even giving examples of grammatically incorrect sentences!

15.8 Grammatical point 8: use of tautologies (redundant / unnecessary language)

The test advice states that in written English, meaning should be expressed 'clearly and concisely', and sometimes less is more. Redundant language refers to information that is expressed more than once in a sentence. In the test, you may see examples of redundant language in the options, and these options should be avoided. Here are some examples of tautologies:

*The track and field events will commence at the **following** times **below**.* ('Following' or ' below', but not both.)

***The reason for this** is **because** he has failed his mock test.* ('Because' and 'the reason for this' are similar in meaning so this sentence can be written as 'The reason for this is that he has failed his mock test' or 'This is because he has failed his mock test'.)

*That is a huge **over-exaggeration**.* (An 'exaggeration' already indicates that it is over the top)

*The meeting took place at **9am in the morning**.*

*Let's write a **short summary** of the first chapter.*

*An **added bonus**.*

*A **new innovation**.*

*An **ATM machine** (the 'M' of 'ATM' already stands for 'machine')*

15.9 Grammatical point 9: choosing the incorrect homophone

Homophones are a problem because they are words which are different in meaning and in spelling, but which have the same pronunciation (hear/here, bear/bare, know/no, mail/male, meat/meet, right/write, wear/where etc.). Here are some of the common ones which could cause problems in the test:

Affect and effect

'Affect' is usually a verb meaning to make a difference to or to influence. *The teacher can affect the outcomes of his students by giving better feedback on their assessments.*

Because 'affect' is a verb, it can exist in other verb forms such as 'affecting' and 'affected'. ('Affect' is also a noun, but you are unlikely to see it as a noun in the test.)

'Effect' is usually a noun. Its definition is a result or consequence of an action. *The number of supply teachers in our school is definitely having an effect on the students.*

'Effect' can be a verb when it means to cause something to happen or to bring about. *The head teacher effected many changes to the behaviour policy.*

'Effective', which comes from the noun 'effect', is an adjective which means that something is producing results.

'Affective' is an adjective which means relating to moods and feelings. It is a word used in the field of psychology, so unlikely to appear in the test, although it could be used in an incorrect answer option.

In the test, assume that if it is a noun, the spelling is 'effect' and if it is a verb, it is 'affect'.

Practice and practise

'Practice' is a noun. *Football practice is on Wednesdays at 4.30pm.*

'Practise' is a verb. *You need to practise your times tables in order to perform well in the mental arithmetic section of the QTS maths test.*

Advice and advise

'Advice' is a noun. *He gave me some excellent advice.*

'Advise' is a verb. *The teacher advised me to sit the foundation tier.*

Its and it's

' It's ' only requires the apostrophe when it means 'it is'. Only use 'its' when the meaning is 'belonging to it'.

It's (it is) *a sunny day today.*

The bag and its contents (the contents of it).

If you see the word ' it's ' as one of the grammar options, ask yourself if it would make sense if the word was replaced by 'it is'. If the sentence does not make sense when you replaced ' it's ' with 'it is', then this is an option that should be immediately discarded. The word ' its' ' does not exist in English, so any examples containing this incorrect spelling should also be eliminated.

There / Their / They're

'There' is used to indicate a place. 'There' is the opposite of 'here', so takes on a similar spelling (you wouldn't write 'heir' or ' hey're ', would you?).

I asked you to sit over there.

It is also used with the verb 'to be' in various tenses for the phrases 'there is', 'there are', 'there were', 'there would be' etc.

'Their' is used to indicate possession and will always be followed by a noun (an object or thing).

Their behaviour is slowly starting to improve.

' They're ' is a contraction (squeezing together) of the words 'they' and 'are'. It is not a contraction of the words 'there are'.

They're going to do a dress rehearsal of 'Macbeth' to the year 7s this afternoon.

If you are not sure which of the three to use, ask yourself whether it would make sense to replace the their / there / they're with the words 'they are'. If the answer is yes, then ' they're ' is the correct option. If the answer is no, then at least you have eliminated ' they're ' as an option and now have to decide between 'there' and 'their'. Now ask yourself if possession is indicated, or check to see if the following word is a noun. If the answer is yes, then use 'their', otherwise use 'there'.

Two / Too / To

'Two' is a number.

'Too' means 'also', 'in addition' or 'excessively'.

'To' is a preposition and should be used when you aren't referring to the number two or a word with the meaning of 'also' or 'excessively'.

Who's / Whose

Do not confuse ' who's ' which is a contracted form for 'who is' with 'whose' (belonging to whom). 'Whose' will normally be followed by a noun (an object or thing) or the word 'is' or 'are' when used as a question word. If you can replace ' who's ' or 'whose' with the words 'who is', then you know that   ' who's ' is correct.

Simon is the boy who's (who is) at risk of permanent exclusion.

Simon is the boy whose parents are coming to see the music teacher. ('Who is' does not make sense in this example.)

Whose is this book? ('Who is' does not make sense in this example.)

Your and you're

This is another extremely high-frequency error in English, with many people using 'your' when they should write ' you're '. ' You're ' is a contracted form for 'you are'. 'Your' is a possessive adjective and will be followed by a noun. If you can replace ' you're ' or 'your' with the words 'you are', then you know that   ' you're ' is correct.

Been / Being

This is a far less common error since these words are not homophones, but still one that can catch a few people out. 'Been' is the past participle of the verb 'to be' and, as such, can only be used with the words 'have', 'has' or 'had' before it. You cannot put these words in front of the word 'being'.

The boy's attitude in the physics lesson had been poor. (It has to be 'been' and not 'being' since there is a 'had' before it.)

15.10   Grammatical point 10: clumsy language

There will be answer options available to you in the test which can be eliminated simply because they do not make sense. These should be relatively easy to spot if you read the answer options with care. Remember that as well as selecting a grammatically correct answer, answers should make sense within the context and should be consistent in style and tone.

You may see answer options where a wrong word has been inserted which is contradictory to the points being made.

John has been making sound progress in maths, and has shown in a recent test that algebra is one of his strong points. For instance, there were some questions on trigonometry which he was unable to answer so this is a topic which will require further revision.

The problem with this example is the words 'for instance'. 'For instance' would make sense if the teacher was going to produce evidence to support the previous statement about John being good at algebra. In the second sentence, the teacher has mentioned some things which John was unable to do, so the second sentence deals with John's maths weaknesses whereas sentence one mentioned his strengths, so there is a contrast between these two sentences, so 'for instance' is not suitable. 'However' or 'On the other hand' would be more appropriate options.

If you are struggling to decipher a given option, then this could be because the statement is non-sensical. If it doesn't make sense, discard it! With answer options of this type, take your time, eliminating the ones which you know are wrong. If it is not obvious what is wrong, then compare the differences from one answer to the next, asking yourself what it is that makes one answer better or worse than the previous one. Here is an example:

a) *Any teacher organising a trip that requires the use of public transport should ensure that there is a ratio of 1 adult with DBS clearance for every 6 students wearing lanyards with emergency contact details, and that all students are equipped with a topped-up travel card.*

b) *Any teacher organising a trip that requires the use of public transport should ensure that there is a ratio of 1 adult with DBS clearance for every 6 students, that all students are equipped and wearing topped-up travel card and lanyards with emergency contact details.*

c) *Any teacher organising a trip that requires the use of public transport should ensure that there is a ratio of 1 adult with DBS clearance for every 6 students, that all students are equipped with a topped-up travel card and that they are all wearing lanyards with emergency contact details.*

d) *Any teacher organising a trip that requires the use of public transport should ensure that there is a ratio of 1 adult for every 6 students with DBS clearance, that all students are equipped with a topped-up travel card and that they are all wearing lanyards with emergency contact details.*

If you were confronted with the above in the test, you might have the following thought process:

When you read answer A, you are not immediately convinced it is a non-sensical answer, but there are one or two things that make you frown while you try to decipher it (frowning is usually a sign that there is a problem). The answer definitely makes sense up to the word 'students' and perhaps makes sense even as far as the word 'lanyards' or 'details'. However, there seems to be a problem with the final phrase as you can't seem to connect the '…and that' sentence to an earlier part of the text. You are not sure about this one. You feel that it is probably not correct, but you won't eliminate it just yet to be on the safe side.

When you read answer B, again, it reads well up to '6 students' but then there are some discrepancies. The answer mentions being 'equipped', but what with? Although it is grammatically correct just to say that students should be 'equipped', surely there should be some guidance or some description as to what being 'equipped' constitutes. It also mentions wearing a travel card which seems rather bizarre. From a grammar and punctuation point of view, it doesn't appear to make sense either as there is an issue with the 'that' clauses. There are only two 'that' clauses, the second of which comes after a comma. Either this second (and final) 'that' clause should come after an 'and' or a third 'that' clause should be added.

Answer C seems to read well and there is consistency with the use of the 'that' statements. This is definitely the best answer so far, and if you compare this to option A, then you feel that answer C is far more likely at this stage.

Answer D seems very similar to statement C. The only difference is the positioning of the words 'with DBS clearance'. In this answer, it reads that it is the students who require the DBS checks and not the teachers, so on this basis, you decide that answer C must be the correct answer.

You may see answer options where the tone of the language has changed. If the text is a letter from a headteacher to parents, it is likely to have a formal and professional tone and is unlikely to contain the phrase 'the behaviour of your son is driving me bonkers, and if it doesn't improve, I'm going to have him chucked out.' If you have eliminated a couple of the options and are not sure which of the remaining two to choose from, look at the tone or look at the length (generally speaking, shorter options are more likely to be more correct than the longer ones, provided they make sense).

Here are a few other grammar points which are worthy of your consideration and could conceivably feature in the test.

Fewer and less

Understanding when to use 'fewer' or 'less' comes down to appreciating whether a word is countable or not countable. Generally, people are more likely to use 'less' when they should say 'fewer', rather than the other way around.

There were fewer boys in the detention than usual. Here we use 'fewer' because you can count boys (one boy, two boys etc.)

There was less participation in the classroom than normal. (Here we use 'less' because you can't count participation (one participation, two participations etc. does not make sense)

Comparatives (more / less ... than) and superlatives (the most / the least)

The problem with comparatives and superlatives is that in English, there are two different ways to form them.

We can form a comparative either by putting the word 'more' or 'less' in front of the adjective, and the word 'than' after the adjective. For certain adjectives (generally ones which are short with one syllable), we simply add '-er' to the adjective.

Simon is more intelligent than Peter. (You would not say *'Simon is intelligenter than Peter.'*)

Simon is shorter than Peter. (You would not say *'Simon is more short than Peter.'*)

A lot of English-speaking people make the mistake of combining the above two rules and end up producing utterances such as:

Simon is more shorter than Peter.

This is completely incorrect! Depending on the adjective you are using, you either use the word 'more' or 'less', or you add the '-er' ending to the adjective.

We can form a superlative either by putting the words 'the most' or 'the least' in front of the adjective. For certain adjectives (generally ones which are short with one syllable), we put the word 'the' before the adjective and add '-est' to the adjective.

Simon is the most intelligent in the class.

Simon is the shortest in the class.

A lot of English-speaking people make the mistake of combining the above two rules and end up producing utterances such as:

Simon is the most shortest in the class.

Again, this is completely incorrect! Depending on the adjective you are using, you either use the words 'the most' or 'the least' with the adjective in its usual form, or you use the word 'the' with an adjective with '-est' at the end.

15.11   Apostrophes

Some options may have incorrect use of apostrophes (see correct apostrophe use in the punctuation chapter). It is possible that you will encounter plurals which have apostrophes or plural words that have apostrophes in the wrong place.

16. Reading comprehension

- Questions: 3-5 based on one text
- Marks: 10-12
- Percentage of paper: 20% - 26%
- Recommended time spent on this paper: 20 - 25 minutes
- What is considered a good mark for this section? 7-9 or above

The reading comprehension section of the QTS test is, without doubt, the hardest part, and is also quite difficult to prepare for. It is essential that you complete the spelling, punctuation and grammar sections quickly and efficiently in order to leave yourself with plenty of time to tackle the reading comprehension, which is also the most time-consuming part of the test.

Even if you are an avid reader, I imagine that it is unlikely that you would choose to read for pleasure the types of text they select for the test, as the texts can be quite heavy-going and difficult to understand. It is very easy to lose concentration while reading articles of this nature, especially when you are reading on screen rather than on paper, as well as reading it under a certain degree of pressure, so it is vital that you give the text your best attention. If you are tired when you take the test, you may find the text especially difficult to focus on, so do make sure that you give yourself the best chance of doing your best by ensuring you have had a good night's rest prior to the test and perhaps have a strong coffee before you enter the test centre!

When you start the reading comprehension text, read the text from start to finish in order to obtain a general gist of what the passage is about. Do not worry about the questions at this stage. If you jump in to the questions too early, skimming and scanning the text for answers, you are definitely not going to perform well. Before tackling the questions, you need to make sure you have read and, more importantly, fully understood the text.

It is quite possible that upon reading the text for the first time, you may not have understood much, but this is completely normal. Read the text again, so that the text starts to make a bit more sense. Remember that reading the text does not simply mean reading the individual words, it means reading and, at the same time, making sense of each sentence and each paragraph, so that as you are reading, you are generating an overall understanding of the passage. With texts of this nature, you will need to read much more slowly and carefully than usual. This is 'deep reading', a process which is under threat as we move into digital-based modes of reading. During your second reading, reread any paragraph that you have not fully understood, not moving on to the next paragraph until you have a clear idea about what you have just read. Once you have read and understood the first few paragraphs, this should set you up well to make better progress with your comprehension of the remainder of the text.

It may take you a good five to ten minutes to read and reread the text before you fully understand it, but this is definitely time well spent. See the time you spend preparing as an investment, because if you know the text well, then there is a good chance that you will be able to answer the questions much more efficiently. You may find that you are able to answer some of the questions without even having to refer back to the text (although I would always suggest checking the text to be on the safe side). Good knowledge of the text will also mean that you can locate the necessary paragraph quickly and efficiently when you are trying to locate evidence for an answer.

In the same way that you will have read the text with attention and care, do the same with the questions. Missing a key word in a question (or in one of the answer options), could have disastrous consequences. You should also read every answer option before choosing your response. If you think the first answer option is the correct one, do not simply select it without even considering the others (other answer options may be more relevant, or the option you thought was correct could be a distractor). Do not use your own prior knowledge to answer questions. All answers options are evidenced in the text, so you do not need to use your own opinion, even if you are convinced that your opinion is better than that of the author!

If there is a certain question that you are struggling with in the text, don't waste too much time on it. Simply move on and come back to it later. It could be that you didn't understand the question because you have not yet gained a full understanding of the text. The question you are struggling with might become less complicated once you have tackled subsequent questions, as the other questions might help unlock extra information which you have missed.

There are certain question types that are likely to appear in the text which I have outlined below. You will not see all of these question types in your test, perhaps only three or four of them.

16.1 Selecting an appropriate title, heading, or sub-heading

You may be asked to choose an appropriate title for the text, or for a given paragraph, from a list of options. In order to select the best heading option, you need to consider the text as a whole. What is the main point of the article? A headline often provides the answer to the key points of the article. For example, the newspaper headline 'Strong universities lessen social tensions' tells us everything we need to know about the article that follows, grabbing our attention and drawing us in (provided that we are interested in education and social issues of course). If you are asked to select a sub-heading for a section or paragraph, then you need to consider what the main points of that section or paragraph only are, rather than the entire text.

Example question (2 marks): select two most appropriate titles for this article:

- Debt collectors employed in state schools
- Cost of school trips spiralling out of control
- Parents asked to cover funding shortfall
- School trips cancelled due to Brexit
- Free education disappearing before our eyes
- Equality in state sector schools at last
- Ofsted says parents to pay for compulsory text books
- Schools requesting parental contributions judged 'outstanding'

16.2   Selecting the audience type for such an article

For this type of question you have to choose the group of people that you think would be most interested and least interested in the article from a list of potential audience types.   Choices could include: headteachers, heads of faculty, Ofsted inspectors, primary school teachers, parents, teachers of a particular subject, or government ministers. This is probably one of the easier question types in theory, although don't rush in with an answer without considering the text as a whole. Just because the headline of the article is 'IT misuse soaring in schools' does not mean that the article is aimed specifically at teachers of IT; the article may be written in a way that means that this is an issue which headteachers, or perhaps teachers in general, should be addressing.

Example question (2 marks): the following groups might all be potential audiences or readers of the article, although some of them would find it more useful than others. Which group would find it the most relevant and which group would find it the least relevant?

- Primary school teachers
- Teachers that organise overseas trips
- Ofsted inspectors
- Parents of school children
- Pastoral staff
- Heads of year
- Headteachers
- Debt collecting agencies

16.3 Selecting a phrase which is closest in meaning to a given phrase from the text

You may be faced with a couple of questions of this type in the text, and these can be quite difficult. Naturally, the phrases you will face are the more complicated phrases in the text containing challenging vocabulary, for example 'the concept of globalisation is stoking social tensions'. However, they do assist you by telling you which paragraph the phrase can be found in, so reread the whole paragraph so that you can see the phrase in an appropriate context. With any luck, however, you may already understand the phrase and not need to refer to the text, simply reading through the answer options until you find the option that you know has the same or similar meaning to the given phrase.

Example question (2 marks): **Select the most appropriate alternative for each phrase as it appears in the context of the passage.**

'their proliferation is hard to ignore' (paragraph 3) is closest in meaning to:

   a)   it is easy to see that they are becoming more popular
   b)   we can't pretend to not see how important they are
   c)   it is difficult to not notice how common they are
   d)   ignoring is difficult due to their decrease

16.4   Selecting statements that accurately convey information in the text

You may be presented with a list of eight statements, from which you have to select four which are true, based on the information in the text. If you have read and understood the text well, then you should be able to quickly select, or exclude, certain options. For any options you are not sure about, you will need to reread the text from start to finish (or, at the very least, the relevant section of the text) in order to confirm if the statement is true or false. If you are unsure about every answer option, then you will potentially need to comb through the text multiple times. Since this could be quite a time-consuming activity, it might be best to abandon this question for now, and move on before returning later, time permitting.

Example question (4 marks): select the four statements that are true:

a) Everybody understands the term 'information literacy'

b) With poor information literacy skills, students may not be able to recognise whether the information they are reading can be trusted or not

c) Information literacy is probably one of the most relevant subjects taught in schools

d) Information literacy helps to assist boys appreciate the relevance of French

e) A good way to promote information literacy is to allow students to use it in an area that interests them

f) Promoting information literacy might result in fewer students submitting plagiarised work

g) Independent learning is rarely underpinned by information

h) The first thing educators need to do is convince people of the need for information before convincing them of the need for information literacy

16.5   Selecting the main points of the text or part of text

This is a very similar question type to selecting statements that accurately convey information, described above.   However, focus on what the main points are, ignoring any statements which may be true, but which are not really pivotal to the text as a whole.

16.6   Completing a list

If the text contains a list of bullet points, you may be asked to complete a list of similar bullet points from a set of options. You need to select the options which are as close as possible in meaning to the original bullet point items in the text. Simply compare the answer options to the bullet points in the list and select the ones which you believe are the same in meaning.

Example question (4 marks): Select the four most appropriate statements to complete the bulleted list which appears in the passage:

In introducing IL (Information Literacy) to students emphasise:

-
- that it helps us in our efforts to retrain in order to ensure continued employability in a changing workplace
-
-
-

a) that it is imperative for us to gain a sound understanding of what is going on in the world
b) that it can help us in our quest to become more educated
c) that there is more to computers than social media
d) that it is imperative to be fluent with everyday packages that are used in business
e) how crucial it is in order for us to make good choices in everyday situations and when making purchases
f) how important it is to improve our general literacy
g) that is enables us to learn more about the things which appeal to us
h) that it enable us to stay on top of current affairs

16.7   Selecting categories for statements

For this question type, you will be given three or four statements which need to be matched to a single word answer or category. This is a drag and drop activity where there are the same number of answers as questions, so is theoretically even easier than a multiple-choice question since every answer option has to be used. You may have four statements which you need to match up to, for example, different education provider types (e.g. secondary schools, primary schools, pupil referral units and universities) so you simply have to decide which of the education providers fits the statement best, again, based on the evidence provided in the text. Additionally, if there are four questions, and you have already worked out three of them and are convinced that they are correct, then the fourth one should automatically be correct by default (although worth checking that this final answer makes sense too and, if it doesn't, that tells you that one of your previous answers is wrong as well).

Example question (3 marks): read the following questions and select which refer to:

- illegality
- irrationality
- procedural impropriety

1. Did the headteacher and / or governing body act outside the scope of their legal powers in taking the decision to exclude?
2. Did the governing board rely on irrelevant points, fail to take account of all relevant points or make a decision so unreasonable that no governing board acting reasonably in such circumstances could have made it?
3. Was the process of exclusion and the governing body's consideration so unfair or flawed that justice was clearly not done?

16.8 Deciding the extent to which a statement is supported by the text if at all

In the test, you will be given some statements and you need to decide if the statement is:

a) **supported** by the text **(S)**
b) **implied** in the text **(I)**
c) **not evidenced** in the text **(NE)**
d) **implicitly contradicted** in the text **(IC)**
e) **explicitly contradicted** in the text **(EC)**

This is definitely one of the harder set of test questions which can sometimes lead to some ambiguous and debatable answers.

If you can point to evidence in the text that supports the statement, then you should choose the 'supported' option. If you can't point to evidence in the text that supports the statement but, reading between the lines, you believe it to be true, then select the 'implied' option.

You will use the 'no evidence' choice if the statement is not supported, implied or contradicted in the text, so if you are struggling with a particular question and feel that guessing is the only option, then the 'no evidence' option might be the most sensible.

If you can point to evidence in the text that disagrees with the statement, then you should choose the 'explicitly contradicted' option. 'Implicitly contradicted' means that there is no direct evidence that disagrees with the statement but, reading between the lines, you believe that the statement is the opposite of the intended meaning of the text.

Example question (4 marks): read the statements below and, based on the evidence provided by the passage, decide whether:

- the statement is **supported** by the text **(S)**
- the statement is **implied** to be the case or is implicitly supported by the text **(I)**
- the text provides **no evidence** or information concerning the statement **(NE)**
- the statement is **implicitly contradicted** or implicitly refuted by the text **(IC)**
- the statement is **explicitly contradicted** or refuted by the text **(EC)**

a) Parents are being asked to make contributions to schools so that schools can buy simple necessities.
b) Some schools that may not be able to afford the essentials have money that is ring-fenced for school trips.
c) Pressure is put on parents so that the payment requests are seen as compulsory rather than optional.
d) Due to Ofsted pressure, schools are effectively writing off some children at a very early age.

16.9   Sequencing pieces of information

A question of this type may appear when the article presents events in a sequence, or the article mentions a process which has several steps. You will have a list of about seven options and you need to select three that are correct. In addition, rather than simply ticking them to confirm that they are correct, you need to state the order that these statements come in by dragging the words 'FIRST', 'SECOND' and 'THIRD' into the answer boxes in order to reflect the order in which the steps are taken.

Example question (3 marks): which of the following are three things a headteacher takes into consideration before an exclusion? Mark them as "FIRST", "SECOND" and "THIRD":

1.   Consider whether appropriate support has been put in place for the pupil
2.   Give the pupil a fidget spinner to assist with concentration
3.   Pupils asked to give their side of the story
4.   Invite the parents or carers in for a meeting
5.   Establish if there are mitigating factors
6.   Ensure that the pupil has served an appropriate number of detentions
7.   Ensure that the pupil is aware of British values

<u>Practice questions</u>

In the mock tests in this book, you will see examples of all nine separate question types.

16.10   Exam Strategy

Here are a few final tips to help you succeed!

First of all, think about what time of day you work best and book a test time that suits you. So, if you are not a morning person, do not book a 9am test. Trying to read and understand a difficult reading comprehension text will not be easy if you aren't at your most alert! Give yourself plenty of time to arrive at the test centre, so that you are relaxed upon arrival. In the build-up to the test, it is preferable to be mentally preparing yourself for the task at hand, rather than to be worrying about whether or not you will arrive in time. If you are sitting the test at a centre that is not in your town, ensure that you have allowed additional time in case of public transport issues or in case the test centre is hard to find. Do bear in mind that the test centres are extremely busy in the month of August since most universities insist that the tests are passed before PGCE courses start in September, so book well in advance, or prepare for a long train ride to a test centre somewhere else in the country!

Prior to the test, you should not need to be doing any last-minute cramming. This is a time to relax and ensure you are as composed as possible. Read some articles from the education section of 'The Guardian' or articles from 'The Times Educational Supplement' to get yourself in the zone. You could even do some revision on the spellings of difficult words.

In the test itself, it is always the spelling that comes first. This part of the test is fairly straightforward and should not take up too much time. You should not be spending a whole minute per question: either you can spell the word or you can't! Don't waste time on the spelling section and look to get through it in about 5 minutes. Don't rush on this section though, but do be efficient. Do remember too that this is the only section in the test which you are not able to revisit.

The second part of the test is the punctuation section, and I would expect most people to pick up quite a few marks immediately and without too much thought. Finding all 15 punctuation omissions might require a bit more consideration, but if you follow my tips in the punctuation section of this book, then you have a systematic way to search for the missing pieces of punctuation. In an ideal word, this section can also be completed very efficiently and, even giving yourself plenty of time to check your work, you should have this section tied up in about 10 minutes. It is definitely worth checking this section, as you may later find that there is a sentence which might need a comma, or a word that might require a hyphen, which might take you from 15 to 16 changes, so you may need some time to think about which piece of punctuation you are then going to remove if you are going to go ahead and make this new change. Remember that this is the most important part of the test as there are always 15 marks available.

The third part of the test is the grammar section. In theory, this is the easiest part since the correct answers have already been given; it is just up to you to find them. In this section, sometimes the answer is obvious, especially if you are a native speaker, so don't worry if some of the questions seem almost too good to be true. Make sure you read the question and the answer options with care, so read slowly, making sure you read every word that is there, and making sure you haven't imagined words that are not there. For some of the more complicated questions, eliminate the obviously wrong answers and then compare the remaining answers. Which parts of the remaining answers are the same and which parts differ? Remember that in each task the questions are linked as they are all part of the same letter or document, so reading the previous question can provide better context for the question you might be struggling with. Again, this section should not take too long, perhaps 10 minutes, and can be returned to if you need to check over any questions you are not sure of.

It is quite possible that by this stage in the test, you have already done enough to secure a pass. However, don't walk out of the test centre just yet! Keep going and complete the reading comprehension (just to be on the safe side!). In my opinion, this is the hardest part of the test to prepare for and the hardest part of the test to take. Ideally, you will have only spent about 20 minutes so far on the other 3 sections, meaning you have over half the remaining time to dedicate to this section. Yes, you have completed 3 out of 4 sections, yes, you have only 10 – 12 more marks available, but in terms of effort, I would see the start of the reading comprehension as the half way point in the test. You will need to spend several minutes simply reading and re-reading the text. Do not worry about the clock ticking - concentrate on the text, try not to let your mind wander, and once you think you have a good understanding of what the text is about, start the questions. Read the questions as carefully as you read the text itself, and read all options when there are multiple-choice possibilities (the 'b' option may look like it's obviously the best answer, but read options 'c' and 'd' as well before committing). Some of the reading comprehension questions will be very challenging, and some of them may not have black and white answers either. However, if you have done your job on the spelling, punctuation and grammar, a few slightly ambiguous questions in the reading comprehension should not derail you too much and you should be leaving the test centre with your 'PASS' certificate!

I hope this book has been of use to you. Do take a look at the QTS Literacy Tutor website at www.qtsliteracytutor.co.uk where there is a free literacy test (different from the 3 mock tests in this book) and other resources to help you prepare for the final exam.

Good luck!

17.   Mock test 1 (45 marks)

Spelling (10 marks)

1. As a _____, Gabrielle will be placed on tutor report from Monday. (consecuence / consiquence / consicuance / consequence)
2. Charlie was a very _____ boy, with plenty of friends. (likable / likeable / likabel / likeabel)
3. The chemistry teacher _____ dropped the bottle of sulphuric acid. (accidentally / acidentaly / accidentaly / accidentelly)
4. To be a successful teacher, you need to be very _____ . (adaptible / adapteble / adaptable / adaptabel)
5. It was _____ that he would never reach his target of a grade 5. (aparent / apparent / apparrant / apparrent)
6. Simon may be quite _____, but he is producing good class work. (mischievious / mischeivous / mischievous / mischeivious)
7. I think the head boy needs to be well-spoken and _____ . (curteous / courteus / courteous / courtious)
8. As a form tutor, it is expected that you provide a _____ for all your tutees. (referance / referrance / reference / referrence)
9. The safeguarding policy needs to be reviewed _____ . (immediatley / imediately / immediatily / immediately)
10. For a three mark question, you are expected to write more than a simple _____ . (sentance / sentanse / sentence / sentense)

Punctuation (15 marks)

What is the new behaviour policy

We have adapted a policy from Chalfont School in wakefield. Chalfont School is a school with a proven track record of outstanding outcomes for their students. The Chalfont students often achieve nearly a grade higher than expectations. The students at Chalfont School are very similar to York Academy students in terms of: prior attainment; comprehensive mix social demographic Free School Meals; and EAL. The new system is based around the use of a planner for rewards and sanctions. Teachers record good work and behaviour in the planner, and they also record poor behaviour in the planner before recording a comment of poor behaviour in class, each student will be reminded of our roles and given an opportunity to make the right choice. Eight recorded instances of poor behaviour in any one week (for incidents which take place inside or outside the classroom will lead a student to be placed in Internal Exclusion. This will give the quiet 90% respite from disruption, making the point that poor behaviour wont be tolerated and must improve.

At the beginning of each week all students start again with a clean slate of zero comments we firmly believe this will allow teachers to teach in a way that will maximise progress allowing students to concentrate on learning in the classroom. We have modified the system and its rules after student and staff input and believe this system will be for the benefit of all

Grammar (10 marks)

Task A

The aim of the MFL department is to:

a) create confident and competent life-long language learners; develop and nurture a curiosity for language learning; embed grammatical awareness which can be applied to English; and developing an appreciation of cultural differences in the world.
b) create confident and competent life-long language learners; develop and nurture a curiosity for language learning; embed grammatical awareness which can be applied to English; and develop an appreciation of cultural differences in the world.
c) create confident and competent life-long language learners; develop and nurture a curiosity for language learning; embed grammatical awareness which can be applied to English; and to develop an appreciation of cultural differences in the world.
d) create confident and competent life-long language learners; to develop and nurture a curiosity for language learning; to embed grammatical awareness which can be applied to English; and to develop an appreciation of cultural differences in the world.

We encourage students to apply their linguistic knowledge to understand and communicate confidently and effectively in a variety of situations. We work as a team

a) to deliver stimulating, challenging and enjoyable lessons that are accessible to all students and which enable them to realise their full potential.
b) for delivering stimulating, challenging and enjoyable lessons that are accessible to all students and which enable them to realise their full potential.
c) to deliver stimulating, challenging and enjoyable lessons that were accessible to all students and which enabled them to realise their full potential.
d) for delivering stimulating, challenging and enjoyable lessons that are accessible to all students and which are enabling them to realise their full potential.

At Kettlewick School, we strongly believe that learning a language can be good fun.

a) Furthermore, the ability to communicate in a foreign language is invaluable when applying for universities and jobs.
b) However, the ability to communicate in a foreign language is invaluable when applying for universities and jobs.
c) Besides, the ability to communicate in a foreign language is invaluable when applying for universities and jobs.
d) On the other hand, the ability to communicate in a foreign language is invaluable when applying for universities and jobs.

Task B

Glasgow Academy has an extremely successful Sixth Form, which has been in the top 10% for value-added for the last ten years. Our primary aim is

a) insuring that all students experience an academic education of the highest standard, and the school would offer a highly supportive environment for students to continue their post-sixteen studies.
b) to ensure that all students experience an academic education of the highest standard, and the school offers a highly supportive environment for students to continue their post-sixteen studies.
c) to insure that all students experience an academic education of the highest standard, and the school offers a highly supportive environment for students to continue their post-sixteen studies.

d) to ensure that all students experience an academic education of the most high standard, and the school offers a highly supportive environment for students to continue their post-sixteen studies.

Girls

a) should be welcome in our Sixth Form,
b) would be welcome in our Sixth Form,
c) might be welcome in our Sixth Form,
d) are welcome in our Sixth Form,

either as part of the consortium or as an external applicant.

In the Sixth Form,

a) we have high expectations, with senior students expected to operate as a role model for students in the lower school.
b) our expectations are high, with senior students expected to operate as role models for students in the lower school.
c) we have high expectations, and we expect senior students to operate as role models for students in the lower school.
d) our expectations are high, with senior students expecting to operate as role models for students in the lower school.

This is reflected in the Sixth Form appearance policy.

a) Boys are expected to dress in a smart business attire, with a suit, tie, and brown or black shoes compulsory. Girls are also expected to dress in a smart business style.
b) Boys are expected to dress in attire, with a smart business suit, tie, and brown or black shoes compulsory. Girls also are expected to dress in a smart business style.
c) Boys are expected to dress in a smart business attire, with a suit, tie, and brown or black shoes compulsory. Girls are also expected to dress in a business style which is smart.
d) Boys are expected to dress in a smart attire for business, with a suit, tie, and brown or black shoes compulsory. Girls are also expected to dress in a smart business style.

Task C

We have just told your child's school that we will inspect it on 13 November 2018. We are writing to you

a) although we would like to know what you think about the school.
b) although we would have liked to know what you think about the school.
c) because we would like to know what you think about the school.
d) because we would like to know what you might think about the school.

You can tell us your views about the school by completing Ofsted's online survey, Parent View.   Parent View asks for your opinion on 12 aspects of your child's school, including

a) the progress made by your child, how good you judge the teaching, and how the school deals with bullying and poor behaviour.
b) the progress your child has made, the quality of teaching, and how the school deals with bullying and poor behaviour.
c) the progress made by your child, the quality of teaching, and what the school does when there is bullying and poor behaviour.
d) the progress made by your child, the quality of teaching, and how the school deals with bullying and poor behaviour.

It also provides a free-text box for you to make additional comments, if you wish. The inspectors will use the online survey responses when inspecting your child's school.

a) Written comments can also be sent to the school in a sealed, confidential envelope, and addressed to the inspection team.
b) Written comments can also be sent to the school, marked confidential and addressed to the inspection team in a sealed envelope.
c) Written comments marked confidential can also be sent to the school in a sealed envelope, and addressed to the inspection team.
d) Written comments can also be sent to the school in a sealed envelope, marked confidential, and addressed to the inspection team.

Reading comprehension (10 marks)

School funding has always been an enormous talking point in the world of politics ever since wholesale reforms were made to the British education system back in 1944 when, due to the abysmal lack of education that many children had received, the government introduced free, and compulsory, education to all up to the age of 15.   However, it seems that in the current financial climate, perhaps using Brexit as an excuse, these 'free' schools are routinely asking for parental contributions in order to compensate for the chronic funding shortfall they are being forced to come to terms with. These parental contributions are not being used to top up teachers' salaries or to build new classrooms, but to spend on the "little extras", as the chancellor, Philip Hammond, in his recent budget described the luxuries our spoilt children enjoy these days – things like the most basic of school equipment: pens, pencils, and exercise books.

It seems that schools are becoming increasingly reliant on these parental offerings with a recent report stating that 43% of parents have been asked to make financial contributions, a figure up from 37% two years ago. Their proliferation is hard to ignore.

Whereas in the past, letters were polite in tone and were simply requesting a token, and obviously voluntary, payment of a couple of pounds per term, some schools are sending letters which resemble the sort of letters you would expect a debt collecting agency to scribe. Letters have been sent asking parents to set up a direct debit of £12.50 per month per pupil, or a one-off payment of £140 per year, making the latter seem like a tantalising bargain. Payment instructions have often been written in bold and underlined type, just to really emphasise the point. What's more, if parents have the audacity to ignore these requests to pay for the 'free' education on offer, failure to pay letters are swift to follow. Some schools have compared their voluntary payment schemes to those of other schools in order to demonstrate how generous their current offer is. What a bargain to only have to pay £450 per academic year for your three children's 'free' education when the school down the road is charging in excess of £500.

How does a school that is reliant on parental contributions, a school that struggles to pay for the basics such as textbooks and interactive whiteboards, meet the increasingly rigorous demands of Ofsted? How does a school in this position expect to keep hold of its most important asset, its teachers, if teachers are unable to deliver high-quality education because it cannot afford the appropriate classroom tools? It has been reported that in some schools, class sizes have increased and certain subjects are no longer offered as they are not profitable, with the result that the Arts, and even modern languages, are no longer on the academic menu because schools are pooling all their resources into the Holy Land of maths, English and science. Children with little hope of passing these subjects have been discarded, being placed into 'sink sets' where they simply fester so that a school can ensure that its higher performers meets the school's required performance data without being held back by the less able.

There has been a long battle about the existence of grammar schools and how they are pooling the best academic talent to the detriment of local comprehensive schools, but in the current climate, exactly the same thing is occurring within local comprehensive schools where intellectual segregation is a reality. A school that can't afford pencils is not going to offer a Duke of Edinburgh Award Scheme or a field trip to Swanage, never mind Iceland.

Some schools are taking things to the other extreme where the most academic pupils are being put on the conveyor belt towards GCSE and A level success and being scrubbed up for top universities. Such pupils are offered myriad opportunities which are simply not available to those not in the club. We have recently seen a school organise a trip to Borneo. Sounds great and, at £3,000 a place, it probably would be. Trips of this nature are only available to the select few, those who can afford to pay, therefore achieving class segregation through seemingly voluntary exclusion.

Nothing can match the trips organised by Eton, however, some of whose pupils went on a red carpet trip to meet President Putin. Not quite the same type of experience as a trip to Dartmoor to measure pieces of granite, but you get what you pay for I guess. The gap between state school pupils and those at the most elite private schools is the biggest inequality of all, with no other country in the world having a bigger equality gap than Britain.

Task 1 (2 marks): select two most appropriate titles for this article:

- Debt collectors employed in state schools
- Cost of school trips spiralling out of control
- Parents asked to cover funding shortfall
- School trips cancelled due to Brexit
- Free education disappearing before our eyes
- Equality in state sector schools at last
- Ofsted says parents to pay for compulsory text books
- Schools requesting parental contributions judged 'outstanding'

Task 2 (2 marks): the following groups might all be potential audiences or readers of the article, although some of them would find it more useful than others. Which group would find it the most relevant and which group would find it the least relevant?

- Primary school teachers
- Teachers that organise overseas trips
- Ofsted inspectors
- Parents of school children
- Pastoral staff
- Heads of year
- Headteachers
- Debt collecting agencies

Task 3 (2 marks): select the most appropriate alternative for each phrase as it appears in the context of the passage.

1. 'their proliferation is hard to ignore' (paragraph 2) is closest in meaning to:

   a) it is easy to see that they are becoming more popular
   b) we can't pretend to not see how important they are
   c) it is difficult to not notice how common they are
   d) ignoring is difficult due to their decrease

2. 'achieving class segregation through seemingly voluntary exclusion' (paragraph 6) is closest in meaning to:

   a) managing to keep students in a class apart by allowing them to rule themselves out
   b) managing to segregate a class by allowing pupils to decide whether or not they want to be in it or not
   c) managing to segregate a class by allowing students to decide whether they should be permanently excluded from school or not
   d) managing to keep students in a school apart if they refuse to volunteer

Task 4 (4 marks): read the statements below and, based on the evidence provided by the passage, decide whether:

- the statement is **supported** by the text **(S)**
- the statement is **implied** to be the case or is implicitly supported by the text **(I)**
- the text provides **no evidence** or information concerning the statement **(NE)**
- the statement is **implicitly contradicted** or implicitly refuted by the text **(IC)**
- the statement is **explicitly contradicted** or refuted by the text **(EC)**

a) Parents are being asked to make contributions to schools so that schools can buy simple necessities.

b) Some schools that may not be able to afford the essentials have money that is ring-fenced for school trips.

c) Pressure is put on parents so that the payment requests are seen as compulsory rather than optional.

d) Due to Ofsted pressure, schools are effectively writing off some children at a very early age.

18.   Numeracy Answers

1.1   I can multiply numbers from 1 to 12 - SKILLS answers

a) 108   b) 24   c) 15   d) 66   e) 60   f) 33   g) 22   h) 176
i) 240   j) 280   k) 126   l) 396   m) 144   n) 396   o) 160   p) 330
q) 576   r) 200

1.2   I can multiply numbers from 1 to 12 - TEST answers

a) 188   b) 144   c) 30   d) 84   e) 66   f) 32   g) 35   h) 27
i) 30   j) 24   k) 66

1.4   I can use the grid multiplication method - SKILLS answers

a) 168   b) 3840   c) 5680   d) 1144   e) 675
f) 4710   g) 57300   h) 26474   i) 457028   j) 696192
k) 45367   l) 413406   m) 1312443   n) 16106100   o) 42482556
p) 488030   q) 6014694   r) 72625896

1.5   I can use the grid multiplication method - TEST answers

a) 28.88   b) 11.04   c) 3660   d) 132   e) 4.2   f) 530
g) 143   h) 125   i) 31.50   j) 1015

1.7   I can multiply by fractions – SKILLS answers

a) $\frac{1}{6}$ b) $\frac{1}{24}$ c) $\frac{1}{18}$ d) $\frac{4}{15}$ e) $\frac{1}{12}$ f) $\frac{2}{7}$ g) $\frac{7}{27}$ h) $\frac{16}{45}$
i) $\frac{36}{49}$ j) $\frac{1}{9}$ k) 15   l) 25   m) 33   n) 25   o) 25   p) 44
q) 22   r) 15

1.8   I can multiply by fractions – TEST answers

a) 315   b) $\frac{3}{14}$ c) 100   d) $\frac{1}{8}$ e) $\frac{3}{25}$ f) 50   g) 200   h) 12

i) 25   j) $\frac{7}{16}$

1.10   I can multiply by decimals – SKILLS answers

a) 0.1	b) 269.7	c) 76.8	d) 2.62	e) 0.25
f) 1	g) 0.0124	h) 0.375	i) 26.24	j) 8.25
k) 39	l) 56.07	m) 31.32	n) 0.9116	o) 36.3268
p) 0.1892	q) 5.4498	r) 4.4368	s) 0.2236	t) 123.662
u) 13.6102	v) 0.004417	w) 0.07326	x) 2.961992	y) 501.800775
z) 22.76912				

1.11   I can multiply by decimals – TEST answers

a) 33   b) 50   c) 70   d) 73.15   e) 35.70   f)13.60

g) 4.30   h) 22.80   i) 9.50   j) 51

2.1   I can perform division using the standard method – SKILLS answers

a) 1.25	b) 1.13	c) 1.5	d) 4	e) 1	f) 3.47
g) 11.25	h) 15.83	i) 9.25	j) 1.67	k) 11.5	l) 30.8
m) 13	n) 24.35	o) 173	p) 112.2	q) 124.5	r) 175.67

2.2   I can perform division using the standard method – TEST answers

a) 48.5   b) 30.5   c) 27.5   d) 34.5   e) 24   f) 2   g) 7.5   h) 2

i) 9   j) 8.5

2.4   I can solve decimal division questions – SKILLS answers

a) 0.3   b) 0.87   c) 2.8   d) 11   e) 8   f) 5

g) 400   h) 10.5   i) 3300   j) 125   k) 5.5   l) 1000

m) 7070   n) 20000   o) 1   p) 350   q) 40   r) 1.43

2.5   I can solve decimal division questions – TEST answers

a) 24300   b) 41235   c) 8230   d) 72900   e) 2743500   f) 52800

g) 12660   h) 45215   i) 2965   j) 20560

3.1   I can simplify fractions – SKILLS answers

a) $\frac{1}{2}$ b) $\frac{1}{9}$ c) $\frac{1}{4}$ d) $\frac{1}{10}$ e) $\frac{1}{6}$ f) $\frac{1}{7}$ g) $\frac{1}{3}$ h) $\frac{1}{5}$

i) $\frac{1}{11}$ j) $\frac{1}{8}$ k) $\frac{1}{12}$ l) $\frac{2}{3}$ m) $\frac{2}{7}$ n) $\frac{2}{5}$ o) $\frac{2}{9}$ p) $\frac{2}{11}$

q) $\frac{3}{5}$ r) $\frac{5}{7}$

3.2   I can simplify fractions – TEST answers

a) $\frac{1}{4}$ b) $\frac{9}{10}$ c) $\frac{5}{7}$ d) $\frac{2}{3}$ e) $\frac{9}{10}$ f) $\frac{3}{4}$ g) $\frac{4}{7}$ h) $\frac{1}{15}$

i) $\frac{1}{15}$ j) $\frac{5}{6}$

3.4   I can convert between fractions, decimals and percentages – SKILLS answers

a) $\dfrac{1}{2}$ = 0.5 = 50%

b) $\dfrac{1}{3}$ = 0.333 = 33.33%

c) $\dfrac{1}{4}$ = 0.25 = 25%

d) $\dfrac{1}{5}$ = 0.2 = 20%

e) $\dfrac{1}{6}$ = 0.167 = 16.67%

f) $\dfrac{1}{7}$ = 0.1429 = 14.29%

g) $\dfrac{1}{8}$ = 0.125 = 12.50%

h) $\dfrac{1}{10}$ = 0.1 = 10%

i) $\dfrac{1}{25}$ = 0.04 = 4%

j) $\dfrac{1}{50}$ = 0.02 = 2%

k) $\dfrac{3}{5}$ = 0.6 = 60%

l) $\dfrac{4}{10}$ = 0.4 = 40%

m) $\dfrac{3}{25}$ = 0.12 = 12%

n) $\dfrac{16}{50}$ = 0.32 = 32%

o) $\dfrac{3}{4}$ = 0.75 = 75%

p) $\dfrac{2}{3}$ = 0.6667 = 66.67%

q) $\dfrac{68}{20}$ = 0.34 = 34%

r) $\dfrac{24}{120}$ = 0.2 = 20%

3.5   I can convert between fractions, decimals and percentages – TEST answers

a) 0.1   b) 90%   c) 0.83   d) 0.33   e) 0.25   f) 87.5%

g) 0.17   h) 0.2   i) 12.5%   j) 10%

3.7   I can calculate a proportion of an amount - SKILLS answers

a) 78.75   b) 52   c) 16.25   d) 84.75   e) 260   f) 260

g) 333   h) 195   i) 49.5   j) 201.25   k) 216.75   l) 273

m) 364.5   n) 7.5   o) 238   p) 270   q) 171   r) 382

3.8   I can calculate a proportion of an amount – TEST answers

a) 16   b) 135   c) £315   d) 45   e) £140   f) £420

g) 70   h) £25   i) 5   j) £20

4.1   I can calculate percentage increase and decrease – TEST answers

a) £1.50   b) 185   c) 83   d) 57   e) 85.5 m   f) 36

g) 11.25   h) 44   i) 162   j) 152

5.2   I can convert between currencies and distances – TEST answers

a) £240   b) ¥884   c) ¥726   d) €1296   e) ¥1908

f) £120   g) £380   h) ¥836   i) €714   j) €572

5.4   I can simplify and divide into ratios – TEST answers

a) 24   b) 150   c) 4   d) 96   e) 20   f) 9   g) 9   h) 14

i) 24   j) 72

6.1   I can solve problems that involve time – TEST answers

a) 2 pm   b) 2hr 35m   c) 12:12 pm   d) 36hr 40m   e) 3.15 pm

f) 3.45 pm   g) 24hr 40m   h) 22hrs   i) 38hr 50m   j) 19hrs

7.1　I can calculate perimeter, area and volume – TEST answers

a) 150 cm

b) 5600000 cm^3

c) 9600 cm^2

d) 7500 cm^2

e) 3200 m^2

f) 3840000 cm^3

g) 2100000 cm^3

h) 18850 m^2

i) 720000 cm^3

j) 580 m

8.2　I can perform multiplication using a calculator – TEST answers

a) £2,782.50

b) £4.14

c) £838.50

d) £62.30

e) £58.84

f) £1,891.93

g) £2,570

8.4　I can perform division using a calculator – TEST answers

a) £2.95

b) 7

c) £115.00

d) Beatrice

e) 5

f) £6.00

g) 21.2m^2

8.6　I can perform compound conversions - TEST answers

a) £4.20 per gallon

b) 0.24 km/m

c) 29.96 mph

d) 4.57 mm/h

e) €2.45

f) 19.3 g/cm^3

g) £5.63 per gallon

9.2   I can work out the mean, median, mode and range – SKILLS answers

	Mean	Median	Mode	Range			Mean	Median	Mode	Range
a)	3	4	4	3	i)		3.18	3.2	NA	2.1
b)	5.4	6	6	3	j)		0.4	0.4	NA	0.8
c)	4.33	4.5	7	6	k)		0.38	0.3	NA	0.9
d)	23.5	11	NA	79	l)		0.64	0.7	0.5	0.3
e)	37.67	21	NA	92	m)		1.5	1.5	1.5	2
f)	24.25	24.5	NA	44	n)		13.68	15	15	20
g)	28.29	29	NA	42	o)		3.30	3	4	4
h)	0.57	1	1	1	p)		2.96	3	5	4

9.3   I can work out the mean, median, mode and range – TEST answers

a)
i) FALSE	ii) TRUE	iii) FALSE	iv) TRUE	v) TRUE	vi) FALSE
vii) TRUE	viii) FALSE	ix) FALSE	x) TRUE	xi) TRUE	xii) TRUE

b)
i) FALSE	ii) TRUE	iii) FALSE	iv) FALSE	v) TRUE	vi) FALSE
vii) FALSE	viii)FALSE	ix) TRUE	x) TRUE	xi) FALSE	xii) TRUE

9.5   I can work out possible values using a summary table – TEST answers

a)
i)TRUE	ii)TRUE	iii)FALSE	iv) TRUE	v)TRUE	vi)TRUE
vii)FALSE	viii)TRUE	ix)TRUE	x) FALSE	xi)TRUE	xii)FALSE

b)
i)FALSE	ii)FALSE	iii)TRUE	iv)FALSE	v)TRUE	vi)TRUE
vii)FALSE	viii)TRUE	ix)TRUE	x)FALSE	xi)TRUE	xii)TRUE

10.2 I can make inferences using a box plot – TEST answers

a)
i)TRUE	ii)TRUE	iii)TRUE	iv)FALSE	v)TRUE	vi)TRUE
vii)FALSE	viii)TRUE	ix)FALSE	x)TRUE	xi)TRUE	xii)TRUE

b)
i)TRUE	ii)TRUE	iii)FALSE	iv)FALSE	v)TRUE	vi)FALSE
vii)TRUE	viii)FALSE	ix)TRUE	x)FALSE	xi)TRUE	xii)TRUE

10.4 I can make inferences using a scatter graph – TEST answers

a)
i)TRUE	ii)FALSE	iii)TRUE	iv)FALSE	v)TRUE	vi)TRUE
vii)FALSE	viii)FALSE	ix)FALSE	x)TRUE	xi)FALSE	xii)TRUE

b)
i)TRUE	ii)FALSE	iii)TRUE	iv)FALSE	v)TRUE	vi)TRUE
vii)FALSE	viii)FALSE	ix)FALSE	x)TRUE	xi)FALSE	xii)FALSE

10.6 I can make inferences using a line graph – TEST answers

a)
i)TRUE	ii)TRUE	iii)FALSE	iv)TRUE	v)FALSE	vi)FALSE
vii)TRUE	viii)TRUE	ix)TRUE	x)FALSE	xi)TRUE	xii)FALSE

b)
i)FALSE	ii)TRUE	iii)TRUE	iv)FALSE	v)FALSE	vi)FALSE
vii)FALSE	viii)FALSE	ix)TRUE	x)FALSE	xi)FALSE	xii)TRUE

10.8 I can make inferences using a bar chart – TEST answers

a)
i)TRUE	ii)TRUE	iii)FALSE	iv)TRUE	v)FALSE	vi)FALSE
vii)FALSE	viii)FALSE	ix)TRUE	x)FALSE	xi)FALSE	xii)FALSE

b)
i)TRUE	ii)FALSE	iii)FALSE	iv)TRUE	v)FALSE	vi)FALSE
vii)FALSE	viii)TRUE	ix)TRUE	x)FALSE	xi)TRUE	xii)FALSE

10.10 I can make inferences using a cumulative frequency graph – TEST answers

a) i)TRUE   ii)FALSE   iii)FALSE   iv)FALSE   v)FALSE   vi)TRUE
   vii)TRUE   viii)FALSE   ix)TRUE

b) i)TRUE   ii)TRUE   iii)TRUE   iv)FALSE   v)FALSE   vi)TRUE
   vii)TRUE   viii)FALSE   ix)TRUE

10.12 I can make inferences using a pie chart – TEST answers

a) i)TRUE   ii)FALSE   iii)FALSE   iv)TRUE   v)FALSE   vi)TRUE
   vii)TRUE   viii)FALSE   ix)TRUE   x)FALSE   xi)FALSE   xii)FALSE

b) i)FALSE   ii)FALSE   iii)TRUE   iv)TRUE   v)TRUE   vi)TRUE
   vii)TRUE   viii)TRUE   ix)TRUE   x)FALSE   xi)FALSE   xii)FALSE

10.14 I can make inferences using a two-way table – TEST answers

a) i)TRUE   ii)FALSE   iii)FALSE   iv)TRUE   v)FALSE   vi)FALSE
   vii)FALSE   viii)FALSE   ix)TRUE   x)TRUE   xi)FALSE   xii)TRUE

b) i)TRUE   ii)TRUE   iii)TRUE   iv)FALSE   v)TRUE   vi)FALSE
   vii)FALSE   viii)TRUE   ix)FALSE   x)FALSE   xi)TRUE   xii)TRUE

11.2 I can work with formulas and weighting – TEST answers

a) Charlie – 63.4   b) 95°C   c) 180.5cm^2 (195.5 – 15)
d) 1.97 siblings   e) Tanya – 77.5   f) 267.947 cm^3
g) 45.8   h) £10,200

11.4   I can work out the best price when considering discounts and offers - TEST answers

a) Super at £18.88

b) E-register saves £823.05

c) Fulltime at £28,500 supply (29,250)

d) Supplier B £9463.86

e) Purchase mower at £1759.20

f) FresherPotatoes £1041.3

g) Purchase £2437

h) ClothingLtd £9721.88

19.   Mock test 1 answers (45 marks, pass mark 30)

Spelling

1. As a **consequence**, Gabrielle will be placed on tutor report from Monday.
2. Charlie was a very **likeable** boy, with plenty of friends.
3. The chemistry teacher **accidentally** dropped the bottle of sulphuric acid.
4. To be a successful teacher, you need to be very **adaptable**.
5. It was **apparent** that he would never reach his target of a grade 5.
6. Simon may be quite **mischievous**, but he is producing good class work.
7. I think the head boy needs to be well-spoken and **courteous**.
8. As a form tutor, it is expected that you provide a **reference** for all your tutees.
9. The safeguarding policy needs to be reviewed **immediately**.
10. For a three mark question, you are expected to write more than a simple **sentence**.

Punctuation (15 marks)

What is the new behaviour policy?   (**Add a question mark since this is a question.**)

We have adapted a policy from Chalfont School in Wakefield (**capital W for Wakefield because this is a place**). Chalfont School is a school with a proven track record of outstanding outcomes for their students. The Chalfont students often achieve nearly a grade higher than expectations. The students at Chalfont School are very similar to York Academy students in terms of: prior attainment; comprehensive mix; (**add semicolon in this complicated list.**

It should be obvious that a semicolon is required and not a comma since the first item has a semicolon after it) social demographic (**add semicolon in this complicated list**) Free School Meals; and EAL.

(**New paragraph as this section talks about how the new system is going to work, while paragraph one is an introduction explaining where the new behaviour policy came from.**) The new system is based around the use of a planner for rewards and sanctions. Teachers record good work and behaviour in the planner, and they also record poor behaviour in the planner. (**Add full stop as the next part is a new idea, so therefore a new sentence.**) Before

(capital B for the start of a new sentence) recording a comment of poor behaviour in class, each student will be reminded of our roles, **(add a comma before coordinating preposition 'and')** and given an opportunity to make the right choice. Eight recorded instances of poor behaviour in any one week (for incidents which take place inside or outside the classroom) **(brackets have been opened but not closed around this extra bit of clarifying information)** will lead a student to be placed in Internal Exclusion. This will give the quiet 90% respite from disruption, making the point that poor behaviour won't **(contraction which requires an apostrophe)** be tolerated and must improve.

At the beginning of each week, **(add a comma after this introductory phrase where the reader can pause for breath)** all students start again with a clean slate of zero comments. **(Add a full stop as this is the end of one idea and the start of a new idea.)** We **(capital letter for the first word of a new sentence)** firmly believe this will allow teachers to teach in a way that will maximise progress, **(add a comma before this additional piece of information where the reader can pause for breath)** allowing students to concentrate on learning in the classroom. We have modified the system and its rules after student and staff input and believe this system will be for the benefit of all. **(Add a full stop at the end of this sentence / paragraph.)**

Grammar (10 marks)

Task A – b, a, a
Task B – b, d, b, a
Task C – c, d, d

Task A

The aim of the MFL department is to:

a) create confident and competent life-long language learners; develop and nurture a curiosity for language learning; embed grammatical awareness which can be applied to English, and developing an appreciation of cultural differences in the world. *(There is no consistency in the verb forms. All the verb forms need to make sense after the word 'to'.)*

b) **create confident and competent life-long language learners; develop and nurture a curiosity for language learning; embed grammatical awareness which can be applied to English, and develop an appreciation of cultural differences in the world.**

c) create confident and competent life-long language learners; develop and nurture a curiosity for language learning; embed grammatical awareness which can be applied to English, and to develop an appreciation of cultural differences in the world. *(Since there is the word 'to' in the question opener, the word 'to' is not required before 'develop'. None of the other verbs are preceded by 'to'.)*

d) create confident and competent life-long language learners; to develop and nurture a curiosity for language learning; to embed grammatical awareness which can be applied to English, and to develop an appreciation of cultural differences in the world. *(Since there is the word 'to' in the question opener, the word 'to' is not required before 'develop', 'embed' and the second 'develop'.)*

We encourage students to apply their linguistic knowledge to understand and communicate confidently and effectively in a variety of situations. We work as a team

a) **to deliver stimulating, challenging and enjoyable lessons that are accessible to all students and which enable them to realise their full potential.**

b) for delivering stimulating, challenging and enjoyable lessons that are accessible to all students and which enable them to realise their full potential. *(It is simply not correct English to say 'for delivering'.)*

c) to deliver stimulating, challenging and enjoyable lessons that were accessible to all students and which enabled them to realise their full potential. *(The present tense should be used because we are talking in general here and not referring to events in the past.)*

d) for delivering stimulating, challenging and enjoyable lessons that are accessible to all students and which are enabling them to realise their full potential. *(It is simply not correct English to say 'for delivering'. The present continuous 'are enabling' is not correct either as we are not talking about what is happening right now, we are talking in general, so the present tense is required.)*

At Kettlewick School, we strongly believe that learning a language can be good fun.

a) **Furthermore, the ability to communicate in a foreign language is invaluable when applying for universities and jobs.**

b) However, the ability to communicate in a foreign language is invaluable when applying for universities and jobs. *('However' does not make sense as this is not a contrasting statement.)*

c) Besides, the ability to communicate in a foreign language is invaluable when applying for universities and jobs. *(You could argue that 'besides' makes sense here, but the word 'furthermore' is better and is also more formal than 'besides', which sounds a bit too informal in this context.)*

d) On the other hand, the ability to communicate in a foreign language is invaluable when applying for universities and jobs. *('On the other hand' does not make sense as this is not a contrasting statement.)*

Task B

Glasgow Academy has an extremely successful Sixth Form, which has been in the top 10% for value-added for the last ten years. Our primary aim is

a) insuring that all students experience an academic education of the highest standard, and the school would offer a highly supportive environment for students to continue their post-sixteen studies. *('Insuring' is not the correct verb. It is the verb 'to ensure' that is needed in this example.)*

b) **to ensure that all students experience an academic education of the highest standard, and the school offers a highly supportive environment for students to continue their post-sixteen studies.**

c) to insure that all students experience an academic education of the highest standard, and the school offers a highly supportive environment for students to continue their post-sixteen studies. *('To insure' is not the correct verb. It is the verb 'to ensure' that is needed in this example.)*

d) to ensure that all students experience an academic education of the most high standard, and the school offers a highly supportive environment for students to continue their post-sixteen studies. *('The most high' is incorrect. This is a one syllable word and would therefore have a superlative form of 'the highest'.)*

Girls

a) should be welcome in our Sixth Form, *(Why 'should'? Is it not certain that they will be welcome?)*

b) would be welcome in our Sixth Form, *(Why 'would'? What needs to happen for them to be welcome?)*

c) might be welcome in our Sixth Form, *(Why 'might'? Is it not certain that they will be welcome?)*

d) **are welcome in our Sixth Form,**

either as part of the consortium or as an external applicant.

In the Sixth Form,

a) we have high expectations, with senior students expected to operate as a role model for students in the lower school. *(The sentence is more or less OK, but 'as a role model' doesn't really work with 'students' in the plural form. 'Our expectations are high' also sounds more formal because it is less personal than 'we have high expectations'.)*

b) **our expectations are high, with senior students expected to operate as role models for students in the lower school.**

c) we have high expectations, and we expect senior students to operate as role models for students in the lower school. *('Our expectations are high' sounds more formal because it is less personal than 'we have high expectations'. The 'and we' is a bit repetitive, so the language here is not very concise.)*

d) our expectations are high, with senior students expecting to operate as role models for students in the lower school. *(The verb form 'expecting' does not make grammatical sense in this sentence.)*

This is reflected in the Sixth Form appearance policy.

a) **Boys are expected to dress in smart business attire, with a suit, tie, and brown or black shoes compulsory. Girls are also expected to dress in a smart business style.**

b) Boys are expected to dress in attire, with a smart business suit, tie, and brown or black shoes compulsory. Girls also are expected to dress in a smart business style. *('To dress in attire' is completely meaningless.)*

c) Boys are expected to dress in a smart business attire, with a suit, tie, and brown or black shoes compulsory. Girls are also expected to dress in a business style which is smart. *('which is smart' does make sense, but this sentence is not concise enough and 'smart business style' would be better English.)*

d) Boys are expected to dress in a smart attire for business, with a suit, tie, and brown or black shoes compulsory. Girls are also expected to dress in a smart business style. *(You can dress in 'smart attire for business' but not in 'a smart attire for business'. Besides 'smart business attire' in option A is far more concise.)*

Task C

We have just told your child's school that we will inspect it on 13 November 2018. We are writing to you

a) although we would like to know what you think about the school. *('Although' is the wrong word to link the two phrases.)*
b) although we would have liked to know what you think about the school. *('Although' is the wrong word to link the two phrases. The visit has not yet happened so the past conditional tense of 'would have liked' makes no sense here.)*
c) **because we would like to know what you think about the school.**
d) because we would like to know what you might think about the school. *(You could argue that this makes sense, but the word 'might' sounds a bit out of place and it is hard to justify that this option sounds better than option C.)*

You can tell us your views about the school by completing Ofsted's online survey, Parent View. Parent View asks for your opinion on 12 aspects of your child's school, including

a) the progress made by your child, how good you judge the teaching, and how the school deals with bullying and poor behaviour. *('How good you judge the teaching' is correct English but 'the quality of teaching' is more concise and more formal.)*
b) the progress your child has made, the quality of teaching, and how the school deals with bullying and poor behaviour. *('The progress your child has made' is correct English but 'the progress made by your child' is more formal.)*
c) the progress made by your child, the quality of teaching, and what the school does when there is bullying and poor behaviour. *('What the school does when there is bullying' is correct English but 'how the school deals with bullying' is more concise and more formal.)*
d) **the progress made by your child, the quality of teaching, and how the school deals with bullying and poor behaviour.**

It also provides a free-text box for you to make additional comments, if you wish. The inspectors will use the online survey responses when inspecting your child's school.

a) Written comments can also be sent to the school in a sealed, confidential envelope, and addressed to the inspection team. *(It is not the envelope that is confidential, but the contents of the envelope.)*

b) Written comments can also be sent to the school, marked confidential and addressed to the inspection team in a sealed envelope. *(The phrase 'marked confidential' needs to be attached to 'envelope' since it is the envelope that is marked confidential.)*

c) Written comments marked confidential can also be sent to the school in a sealed envelope, and addressed to the inspection team. *(It is the envelope and not the written comments that need to be marked confidential.)*

d) **Written comments can also be sent to the school in a sealed envelope, marked confidential, and addressed to the inspection team.**

Reading comprehension (10 marks)

Task 1 answers

Parents asked to cover funding shortfall
Free education disappearing before our eyes

Task 2 answers

Headteachers – most relevant
Debt collecting agencies – least relevant

Task 3 answers

1 – c
2 - a

Task 4 answers

a) S b) NE c) S d) I